Coming Forth as Gold

Coming Forth as Gold

Jenny Hill

WESTBOW
PRESS®
A DIVISION OF THOMAS NELSON
& ZONDERVAN

WestBow Press books may be ordered through booksellers or by contacting:

WestBow Press
A Division of Thomas Nelson & Zondervan
1663 Liberty Drive
Bloomington, IN 47403
www.westbowpress.com
1 (866) 928-1240

ISBN: 978-1-9736-7439-9 (sc)
ISBN: 978-1-9736-7438-2 (e)

Print information available on the last page.

WestBow Press rev. date: 10/3/2019

New Beginnings

———◆◆◆———

"Forget the former things; do not dwell on the past. See, I am doing a new thing. Now it springs up; do you not perceive it? I am making a way in the wilderness and streams in the wasteland." Isaiah 43:18-19 (NIV)

Today is a new day and a new year. God is blessing you with the chance to start fresh. He is giving you another chance to become the person He created you to be. Make the most of this year. Allow it to be one of your better years. Chase your dreams and decide that you are valuable to God. You're worth so much more than you realize. It's time to let Jesus into your heart because He is the key to your freedom. Your past is no longer your prison. Find out what God's true purpose is for your life. Give Him all of your fears, worries, and anxieties to heal. If you're not sure where to start, then ask God. Trust Him to guide you through His Holy Spirit. Have a Happy New Year and many blessings to you.

JANUARY 2ND

Prosper Me

———◦◇◦———

"For I know the plans I have for you," declares the Lord, "plans to prosper you and not to harm you, plans to give you hope and a future." Jeremiah 29:11 (NIV)

Don't be afraid to become what God called you to be. He will take you by the hand and guide you toward your purpose. Jesus is a great Master and Teacher. Whenever you take a test in school, the teacher is right there in the classroom. They stay silent until the students are finished, but they are still with you while you take the test. Jesus is the same way. He teaches you how to do something, then you take the test. When He is silent, it doesn't mean He's not there. He is seeing how well you apply what He has taught you. If you fail, He is right there waiting to pick you up and dust you off so you can try it again. Don't quit.

Restoration

———◆———

"The thief cometh not, but that he may steal, and kill, and destroy: I came that they may have life, and may have it abundantly." John 10:10 (ASV)

Satan may have taken everything from you. He tries to hurt you, your family, and the people you love. He wants to take as much as he can to make you curse God. He doesn't want you to live in peace so he will slowly ease his way in until you are miserable or dead. But God has sent us a Savior. He sent His own Son, Jesus. He has come to restore everything Satan has stolen from you. Jesus came so that He could give you more than you could ever imagine. God has already won the victory.

JANUARY 4TH

Surrender

———◆———

"And Jesus looking upon them saith, 'With men it is impossible, but not with God: for with God all things are possible." Mark 10:27 (KJV)

We often try to live our lives on our own separate from God, taking on tasks in the flesh. We wear ourselves out very quickly until we are ready to give up. Eventually we realize that without God's help, there are some things that are impossible for us to accomplish by ourselves. Ask God for His help because He is all powerful. He can do anything you ask Him to do and so much more. Don't be afraid when you hear the word, "surrender." It doesn't mean you are giving up. Surrendering your life to Jesus means that you are giving up your old life for a new life with Him. He will take all the old desires from you and give you new desires which will change your life forever. You will feel a love and a peace that truly surpasses all understanding. You will receive perfect peace within you that no circumstance will be able to take from you.

Peace

———◆———

"Peace I leave with you, My peace I give unto you: not as the world giveth, give I unto you. Let not your heart be troubled, neither let it be afraid." John 14:27 (KJV)

There is not one person on this earth who does not experience some kind of trouble or pain throughout their lifetime. Trials come to make you stronger. They help you grow. Jesus teaches us not to be afraid. Through Christ you can still experience peace in your troubles because you know that He is right there going through it with you. Stay in peace knowing that when trials come, it means you are getting ready to go into the next level of your life. You will get through this storm and be strengthened for the new level.

Resurrected

———◆———

"And when He thus had spoken, He cried with a loud voice, 'Lazarus, come forth.' And he that was dead came forth, bound hand and foot with graveclothes: and his face was bound about with a napkin. Jesus saith unto them, 'Loose him, and let him go.'" John 11:43-44 (KJV).

Jesus has the power to resurrect the dead. Before you came to Christ, you were dead in your sins. You were a prisoner, but Christ brought you back to life and freed you. Jesus took away all your sins, cleaned you up, and gave you freedom from your enemies. Remain in Him. Do not resist the change God is doing in your life. It may get scary at times, but if you stay close to Jesus He will not let you fall. Trust Him fully.

Come Home

———◆———

"Let us search and try our ways, and turn again to the Lord."
Lamentations 3:40 (KJV)

You are a fleshy being born into sin so it can be difficult not to backslide at times. Take a good look at your life and ask yourself, "Am I doing what Jesus would do or am I living my life in sin?" If you are living in sin, ask God for forgiveness and turn back to Him for guidance. Ask Him to reveal His will for your life. Do not be afraid. You can do this as long as you remain at His feet.

Focus

———◆———

"For what shall it profit a man, if he shall gain the whole world, and lose his own soul?" Mark 8:36 (KJV)

God should always be your main focus. He provides you with everything you need if you remain in Him. Whatever you focus on will grow. If your main focus is on financial gain or on what people think, then that is what will eventually control you. It will take your focus away from God. The devil will creep in very smoothly leaving you feeling miserable and empty. The worst part is spending an eternity in Hell if you fall into Satan's trap. Ask yourself, "Is it really worth it?" Put God first and He will add everything you need.

Protection

———⟨◆⟩———

"He that dwelleth in the secret place of the Most High shall abide under the shadow of the Almighty. I will say of the Lord, "He is my refuge and my fortress: my God; in Him will I trust." Psalm 91:1-2 (KJV)

When you are a child of God, He will hide you away in His secret place away from any evil. No weapons of the devil will prosper against you. God will keep you covered from your enemies. Put all your trust in God and know that everything is happening for a reason. He uses the good and the bad to grow you into a stronger person. Allow God to continue fighting your battles and trust Him. He is with you wherever you go. He is with you right now.

Blessed

———◆———

"Blessed are ye, when men shall revile you, and persecute you, and shall say all manner of evil against you falsely, for My sake. Rejoice, and be exceeding glad: for great is your reward in Heaven: for so persecuted they the prophets which were before you." Matthew 5:11-12 (KJV)

Jesus wants you to realize how blessed you are when people say things about you because you chose to follow Him. People will say unpleasant things about you when you are a child of God because they may not understand. It's up to you to help them understand. Jesus teaches you to be glad when you are persecuted because you have a great reward in Heaven waiting on you for your sacrifice. Always remember that Jesus was persecuted first, but He was also glorified by the Father. If you suffer with Christ, you will also be glorified with Christ.

Life

———◆———

"In the last day, that great day of the feast, Jesus stood and cried, saying, 'If any man thirst, let him come unto me, and drink. He that believeth on me, as the scripture hath said, out of his belly shall flow rivers of living water." John 7:37-38 (KJV)

Jesus will not make anyone come to Him. He is giving you the choice to come to Him. If you are becoming tired and feeling empty, ask Him to fill you with His power. Ask Him for strength. You can do nothing apart from God. Eventually, you will feel worn out. Jesus teaches us that whoever believes in Him will have life and they will have it more abundantly. Life will flow from within you and will overflow into the lives of those God places around you giving others hope.

Spiritual Warfare

———◆◆◆———

"For we wrestle not against flesh and blood, but against principalities, against powers, against the rulers of this world, against spiritual wickedness in high places. Therefore take unto you the whole armour of God, that ye may be able to withstand in the evil day, and having done all, to stand."
Ephesians 6:12-13 (KJV)

Satan was thrown out of Heaven because he wanted to be God. He is now spending eternity in Hell and he is trying to take as many souls as he can with him. You are in a spiritual war. Your fight is not with people. You're being fought over by God and Satan. Don't be deceived. Heaven is real and so is Hell. Prepare yourself for the day of judgement because it is coming. Please choose life.

Sacrifice

———◆———

"But when He saw the multitudes, He was moved with compassion on them, because they fainted, and were scattered abroad, as sheep having no shepherd. Then saith He unto His disciples, 'The harvest truly is plenteous, but the labourers are few; Pray ye therefore the Lord of the harvest, that He will send forth labourers into His harvest." Matthew 9:36-38 (KJV)

Jesus showed us great compassion even though we didn't deserve it. He sacrificed Himself for us while we were still in sin and He was innocent. There are many people still lost with no one to help them. Sacrifice your time to help others the same way Christ helped you. Do something meaningful to help someone else today.

Ask

---◆---

"For every one that asketh receiveth; and he that seeketh findeth; and to him that knocketh, it shall be opened." Luke 11:10 (KJV)

Jesus teaches us that if we ask to receive Him, we will. If you are wanting answers just ask Him and you will receive them. Jesus won't force Himself or His teachings on anyone. You have to really want it for yourself. No one starts out with all the answers. You have to ask Jesus for guidance. Once you knock on the door of Jesus, He will open it and He will teach you Himself. He wants you to come as you are. Not one of us is perfect except for Jesus. He knows exactly who you are already so don't be afraid or ashamed to come to Jesus. He is our Savior.

JANUARY 15TH

Real Love

"Nay, in all these things we are more than conquerors through Him that loved us. For I am persuaded, that neither death, nor life, nor angels, nor principalities, nor powers, nor things present, nor things to come, nor height, nor depth, nor any other creature, shall be able to separate us from the love of God, which is in Christ Jesus our Lord." Romans 8:37-39. (KJV)

How awesome is that? There is nothing in ALL creation that can stop God from loving you. Our Heavenly Father, our Creator, actually came down from His throne in Heaven to become a human. He lived with us and taught us how to live righteously. He suffered and died for us. He made an exchange with us. He took our sin (death) and gave us His righteousness (life). Now that's real love.

Pure Heart

———◆———

"Flee also youthful lusts: but follow righteousness, faith, charity, peace, with them that call on the Lord out of a pure heart." 2 Timothy 2:22 (KJV)

Jesus teaches us to stay away from evil desires. We are all naturally sinful. You can't avoid evil thoughts from entering your mind, but don't entertain the thoughts. Immediately cast them down. When you call on Jesus to help you, He fills you with His power to resist evil desires. When you resist the devil, he flees from you. Continue to trust God, love others, do the next right thing, and remain in perfect peace. Keep people around you with good and pure hearts that you can truly trust. Whoever you keep around you is who you start to become.

JANUARY 17ᵀᴴ

Salvation

———⊷◆⊶———

"For I am not ashamed of the gospel of Christ: for it is the power of God unto salvation to every one that believeth; to the Jew first, and also to the Greek." Romans 1:16 (KJV)

There are people who may persecute you, criticize you, or tease you about being a follower of Jesus Christ. There is no reason to be ashamed or embarrassed about what Jesus did for you on the cross. He hung on a cross in front of many people without any shame to save you from eternal darkness and death. He humbled Himself to die for all of humanity even though He had no sin in Him. He has saved many of us from our own destruction and has given eternal life to those who choose to have it. How could anyone be ashamed to be loved that much by God? You are blessed.

Be Alert

"Therefore rejoice, ye Heavens, and ye that dwell in them. Woe to the inhabiters of the earth and of the sea. For the devil has come down unto you, having great wrath, because he knoweth that he hath but a short time." Revelation 12:12 (KJV)

Satan was kicked out of Heaven for sowing discord among some of the angels. He and those fallen angels are now here on earth trying to destroy God's children because that is the only way he can hurt God. He is angry and moving very quickly to deceive you because he knows that Jesus is coming soon. Stay sober and alert because the devil is very smooth. As soon as you let your guard down, he will move in with his tricks and deception. Don't be fooled. No one knows the day or the hour Jesus is coming so make sure you're ready. Stay close to God.

JANUARY 19TH

Spread the Message

———⊰⬧⊱———

"Now the man out of whom the devils were departed besought Him that he might be with Him: but Jesus sent him away, saying, 'Return to thine own house, and shew how great things God hath done unto thee.' And he went his way, and published throughout the whole city how great things Jesus had done unto him." Luke 8:38-39. (KJV)

Jesus healed a man who was possessed by demons. The man was so grateful and asked to follow Jesus, but Jesus told him to go home so he could tell everyone else what He did for him. The reason you face trials and tribulations is so that God can show Himself strong through you. After all the devil did to try and stop you, you're still here. God healed you so others could see how real, loving, and faithful He is. Allow God to use you to bring others into His Heavenly Kingdom.

Vengeance

—◆—

"Dearly beloved, avenge not yourselves, but rather give place unto wrath: for it is written, 'Vengeance is mine; I will repay,' saith the Lord. 'Therefore if thine enemy hunger, feed him; if he thirst, give him drink: for in so doing thou shalt heap coals of fire on his head. Be not overcome of evil, but overcome evil with good." Romans 12:19-21 (KJV)

Jesus teaches us not to get revenge on anyone. If someone does something to hurt you, don't get even. God makes it very clear that when you are His child, He will avenge you. Do not let anyone push you to the point of doing evil. Continue to do what you know is right and God will take care of your enemies. Most importantly, God will take care of you. Stay strong in our Heavenly Father because He will not forsake you.

God's Example

"Be ye therefore followers of God, as dear children; And walk in love, as Christ also hath loved us, and hath given Himself for us as an offering and a sacrifice to God for a sweet smelling savour." Ephesians 5:1-2 (KJV)

We are children of God. He is our Father in Heaven. God blessed us with an example of how to live our lives. He wants us to walk in love like Jesus Christ and sacrifice the way Jesus did for us. Sacrificing some of your time to help someone else today will increase your love, joy, and peace. We need to really love each other and be there for one another. You never know the last time you will see someone so don't regret anything.

Free Indeed

—◆—

"If the Son therefore shall make you free, ye shall be free indeed." John 8:36 (KJV)

Jesus Christ died to free you from a life of sin and to give you eternal life. Come boldly to His throne and ask Him for forgiveness. We are sinful by nature, so it's not possible to be perfect all the time, but strive to be better everyday. You may fall short at times, but God will pour out His grace over you. If you fall, ask God for forgiveness, get back up, learn from your mistakes, and keep moving toward better. When you accept Jesus Christ as your Lord and Savior, He sets you free from a life of sin. Once you are set free, you will no longer be controlled by sin. Do not be Satan's slave. Walk in the gift God gave you... FREEDOM.

Righteous

—————◆—————

"And the scripture was fulfilled which saith, Abraham believed God, and it was imputed unto him for righteousness: and he was called the Friend of God." James 2:23 (KJV)

When you believe God's promises, you are considered a righteous person. You are called God's friend. Jesus teaches that the prayers of a righteous person are answered. God is the best friend you could ever have so don't ignore Him. Talk to Him because He is listening and waiting to answer your prayers. Keep your faith in God and also believe in yourself because it's equally important. Build up your confidence and know that as a child of God, no weapon formed against you shall prosper.

Do Good

———◦◆◦———

"Marvel not at this: for the hour is coming, in which all that are in the graves shall hear His voice, And shall come forth; they that have done good, unto the resurrection of life; and they that have done evil, unto the resurrection of damnation."
John 5:28-29 (KJV)

Jesus will be coming back soon and when He does, He will collect the people who do good. God will give eternal life to the righteous and reward them. Don't stop doing what is right. You get what you give so don't follow the ways of the wicked which leads to eternal death. When you let God lead the way, you receive an unexplainable strength. Your peace and joy grows more and more everyday. Stay close to God, love Him, and love others. The more you draw close to God, the closer He draws to you.

Take Heart

———◆———

"These things I have spoken unto you, that in me ye might have peace. In the world ye shall have tribulation: but be of good cheer; I have overcome the world." John 16:33 (KJV)

Troubles, trials, and tribulations will come to you in this world. None of us are living a trouble free life. Everyone has their own troubles and battles to fight, but Jesus gives a peace that surpasses all understanding. If you remain in God, He will bless you with strength and peace in the midst of any battle you are facing. He gives you hope and He comforts you by reminding you that there is nothing to be afraid because He wins in the end. Remain at the feet of Jesus and He will protect you from your enemies.

Healing

"When he heard that Jesus was come out from Judaea into Galilee, he went unto Him, and besought Him that He would come down, and heal his son: for he was at the point of death."
John 4:47 (KJV)

Jesus wants you to come to Him for any help you may need. If you or someone you know needs healing, come boldly to Him and ask Him. Jesus loves to show Himself strong. Whenever you or a loved one becomes ill, don't hesitate to ask Him for healing. Sometimes God will allow you to go through things that are uncomfortable so He can get your attention. You realize how real Jesus is and how much you need Him when you experience painful situations. You learn to depend on Him in everything once you experience His healing power.

Love Everyone

———◆———

"For if ye love them which love you, what thank have ye? for sinners also love those that love them. And if ye do good to them which do good to you, what thank have ye? for sinners also do even the same." Luke 6:32-33 (KJV)

Jesus teaches that when you love those and are good only to those who you love, then you do not get credit for that. People who are evil also love those who love them. People will recognize that you are a child of God by the way you treat others. If you're able to love all people and be good to all people regardless of what they do to you, it means you're growing as a child of God. It's not easy to turn the other cheek, but it's necessary if you want to get to the right place in life. God will reward you for keeping in peace with everyone no matter how they treat you. These are the situations that strengthen you as a person.

Working for God

---◆---

"And whatsoever ye do, do it heartily, as to the Lord, and not unto men; Knowing that of the Lord ye shall receive the reward of inheritance: for ye serve the Lord Christ." Colossians 3:23-24 (KJV)

Jesus teaches that when you are led to do something, you need to put your whole heart into it. Your reward will come from our Father in Heaven, not from people. It doesn't matter what anyone else thinks because they are not in charge of your destiny. God is your master, not humans. If God leads you to something, make sure that you are working at it with all you got to please God. You are not here to please people, but you are here to serve the Lord.

Faith and Works

———◆———

"For as the body without the spirit is dead, so faith without works is dead also." James 2:26 (KJV)

If you say you have faith, but you don't do any good deeds, then your faith is dead. You can't say you believe in Jesus, but not serve Him. Doing good deeds and serving Christ whenever He asks you to do something is a great way to show that you trust God. Your faith in God will be known to others when they see you doing good to all people. Show your gratitude to God for all He has done for you by taking direction from Him. When you show gratitude for the things you have, even the little things, God blesses you with a lot more. Your faith will grow as you serve God and His people. Go wherever God leads you and do whatever God asks you to do.

Love and Encourage

———◆———

"And let us consider one another to provoke unto love and to good works: Not forsaking the assembling of ourselves together, as the manner of some is; but exhorting one another: and so much the more, as ye see the day approaching." Hebrews 10:24-25 (KJV)

Jesus teaches that we ought to encourage one another through love and good deeds. We need to come together and help one another. We need to flock together as children of God, especially as the end times are approaching. Look at some of the things happening around the world. We don't have as much time as we think we do. It's time for us to pull together as one big family encouraging and loving one another. We are stronger together.

Save Us

———◆———

"And when He was entered into a ship, His disciples followed Him. And, behold, there arose a great tempest in the sea, insomuch that the ship was covered with the waves: but He was asleep. And His disciples came to Him and awoke Him, saying, 'Lord, save us: we perish.' And He saith unto them, 'Why are ye fearful, O ye of little faith?' Then He arose, and rebuked the winds and the sea; and there was a great calm." Matthew 8:23-26 (KJV)

You will face your own kinds of storms in life, but Jesus wants you to keep faith. There is no need for you to be afraid in any storm because Jesus is right here with you. Don't allow the harder times keep you from reaching your destination. It might feel scary at times, but keep in mind that Jesus is never going to leave you to face any storms alone. Storms will rise up to test your faith, but remain in Christ and He will not allow you to drown.

FEBRUARY 1ˢᵀ

Names in Heaven

———⬥———

"He replied, 'I saw Satan fall like lightning from Heaven. I have given you authority to trample on snakes and scorpions and to overcome all the power of the enemy; nothing will harm you. However, do not rejoice that the spirits submit to you, but rejoice that your names are written in Heaven." Luke 10:18-20 (NIV)

Satan fell from Heaven. Now he roams the earth looking for whom he may devour, but God has given you the power to overcome the enemy. God gave you power to make spirits submit to you. If you are a child of God, there is nothing that can harm you. Don't be afraid when you're under attack, use the power within you to overcome all the enemy throws at you. It's exciting to know that God has given you authority over your enemies, but rejoice even more knowing that your name is written in Heaven.

Do Not Worry

———◆———

"Who of you by worrying can add a single hour to your life? Since you cannot do this very little thing, why do you worry about the rest?" Luke 12:25-26 (NIV)

Walk forward toward your purpose in faith, believing that Jesus will provide all you need along the way. Worrying about something constantly can't change a thing and it will not add any time to your life. It actually takes time from your life and it keeps you from accomplishing the tasks before you. You can't ever get back that time back again. Don't waste your time worrying about something you can't control. Instead, enjoy every moment you are blessed with and be as present as you possibly can. Jesus tells us not to worry about anything. Focus on God and the rest will fall into place. Have faith in God because He can do the impossible.

God Increase

———◦◇◦———

"He must increase, but I must decrease. He who comes from above is above all; he who is of the earth is earthly and speaks of the earth. He who comes from Heaven is above all. And what He has seen and heard, that He testifies; and no one receives His testimony. He who has received His testimony has certified that God is true." John 3:30-33 (NKJV)

When you decided to follow Jesus, you became more like Him. You gave Him your old life in exchange for a new life in Him. Continue to put away your old ways so that He can increase within you and be shown strong through you. God came down from Heaven through Jesus to show you how to live. He gave you free will to choose His way or the world's way. When you decided to accept Him and receive His testimony of Heaven, He blessed you. You are a person who truly experiences God and the blessings that come with being a child of God.

FEBRUARY 4TH

Secret Things

——◆◆◆——

"He reveals deep and secret things; He knows what is in the darkness, and light dwells with Him." Daniel 2:22 (NIV)

There is no one on this earth that can hide from God or hide what they do. God sees everything. He will reveal the secret things that we may try to cover up. Whenever we do anything in the dark, eventually it comes to light. God is light so wherever His presence is, no darkness can remain there. Keep working hard to renew your heart and spirit because we can't trick God. You will be judged for everything you decide to do when the end comes. You will be greatly rewarded for the good you do on earth. Do your best to please God and not people. Love God first and He will take care of everything else.

FEBRUARY 5TH

Sanctification

———◦◦———

"May God Himself, the God of peace, sanctify you through and through. May your whole spirit, soul, and body be kept blameless at the coming of our Lord Jesus Christ." 1 Thessalonians 5:23. (NIV)

Our Father in Heaven is a Father of Peace. He only wants the best for His children. He wants us all to stay in peace. He loves to pick us up, clean us up, and make us good inside and out. Jesus will be coming soon. When He comes, He wants to find you good and blameless. There is not one child He wants to throw away. He wants to save us all which is why He has given us so much time to get it right. Don't hesitate to grow and learn from your past mistakes. Hard times come to strengthen you and teach you how to become a better person. When Jesus comes back, make sure you are counted as one of His children with a good and pure heart.

God is with you

———◆———

"Have I not commanded you? Be strong and courageous. Do not be terrified; do not be discouraged, for the Lord your God will be with you wherever you go." Joshua 1:9 (NIV)

God commands all of His children to be strong and courageous. He will be with you wherever you go. There's no reason to be afraid or fear anything. Our Father in Heaven is in charge of your destiny. What will be will be. Since we cannot control what will happen in life, enjoy it to the fullest remembering our Heavenly Father is with you wherever you are.

Plentiful

———◆———

"You will have plenty to eat, until you are full, and you will praise the name of the Lord your God, who has worked wonders for you; never again will my people be shamed." Joel 2:26 (NIV)

God does amazing things for His children. He will save you from your adversaries. He will never let you be shamed again by the enemy if you stay close to Him. God will overflow you with everything you need. When you continue to follow Him and be grateful for all He blesses you with, He will give you more than you need. He only wants the very best for His children. You are in His royal family. He will never forsake you. He loves to bless you, but He wants you to ask Him for whatever it is that you want, just ask.

FEBRUARY 8TH

Hiding Place

———❖———

Thou art my hiding place; thou shalt preserve me from trouble; thou shalt compass me about with songs of deliverance." Psalm 32:7 (KJV)

God will hide you from the rain. He will protect you from anything or anyone that may rise up against you. He will deliver you from the enemy. Do not be afraid of anything. Your Father in Heaven will keep you safe underneath His wings. Life is not always going to be easy, but keep your eyes on Him and He will take care of you in the midst of any storm. Do not be discouraged.

Jesus Sacrifice

———◦◆◦———

"For God so loved the world, that He gave His only begotten Son, that whosoever believeth in Him should not perish, but have everlasting life." John 3:16 (KJV)

God is love. He gave His only Son to keep you from perishing and to save you from eternal darkness. How could you not be grateful? God sacrificed Jesus so that you could have a relationship with Him while you are still here on this earth. He also made a way for you to have eternal life with Him. There is nothing left to say, but thank You.

Confess

—◆—

"But what saith it? The word is nigh thee, even in thy mouth, and in thy heart: that is, the word of faith, which we preach; That if thou shalt confess with thy mouth the Lord Jesus, and shalt believe in thine heart that God hath raised Him from the dead, thou shalt be saved." Romans 10:8-9 (KJV)

Don't take a chance with your life. Be wise and know where you are going after your life in this world is done. It doesn't take a lot to become a child of God and to reserve your place in the Heavenly Kingdom. All you need to do to have eternal life is confess with your mouth that Jesus is Lord and believe in your heart that He was raised from the dead. Make sure you'll be saved when your life here on earth is finished. Do not be deceived by anyone or anything. Heaven is real.

Rise Again

"Lay not wait, O wicked man, against the dwelling of the righteous; spoil not his resting place: For a just man falleth seven times, and riseth up again: but the wicked shall fall into mischief." Proverbs 24:15-16 (KJV)

Jesus came to save you because you aren't perfect. He died in your place to take on your sins and to give you His righteousness in exchange. The righteous will fall at times, but they get back up. Whenever the righteous rises again, they are wiser and stronger than they were before their fall. The wicked stumbles and stays down instead of learning from their mistakes. If your brother or sister falls, reach out your hand and help pull them back up. Don't be like the wicked who kick their brother or sister while they're down. The wicked will wait for you to fall in order to criticize you. You will know the wicked by their fruit. Be watchful of the wicked. If you slip, get back up. Continue moving forward as you grow from your fall.

FEBRUARY 12ᵀᴴ

Light of Life

———◆◆———

"Then spake Jesus again unto them, saying, 'I am the light of the world: He that followeth Me shall not walk in darkness, but shall have the light of life." John 8:12 (KJV)

Jesus will come and find you in the darkest part of your life. He will give you a chance to follow Him, but He will not make you. He gives you the choice to come out of your old path of darkness which leads to eternal death or to choose a new path of light which leads to eternal life. When you choose to follow Him, He will show you a new way and bless you with a new perspective on life. Things will start to make a lot more sense and your life will be changed forever.

The Vine

———◆———

"I am the vine, ye are the branches: He that abideth in Me, and I in him, the same bringeth forth much fruit: for without Me ye can do nothing." John 15:5 (KJV)

Jesus teaches that you are to stay close to Him. He makes it clear that without Him, you cannot do anything. There are people who reach a certain point in life where things get so hard for them that they don't want to go on anymore. Some commit suicide, some drown their sorrows with drugs and alcohol, and some get into trouble which can lead to death. When you come to this crossroads, you have to decide which path you will take. Will you continue to suffer until death or will you choose to enjoy life in Christ? There is only one path to eternal life and that path is JESUS. If you get lost on your journey, call out to Jesus and He will show you the way.

God is Just

———◆———

"For God is not unrighteous to forget your work and labour of love, which ye have shewed toward His name, in that ye have ministered to the saints, and do minister." Hebrews 6:10 (KJV)

Our Heavenly Father is a very fair and just King. He loves to see His children helping others when they are in need. He wants us to come together as one big family, loving and helping one another to succeed. He sees everything you do and He knows your heart. He will not forget all you have done in His Kingdom. He will reward you for all that you do in His royal family.

Inner Light

———◆———

"Ye are the light of the world. A city that is set on an hill cannot be hid. Neither do men light a candle, and put it under a bushel, but on a candlestick; and it giveth light unto all that are in the house. Let your light so shine before men, that they may see your good works, and glorify your Father which is in Heaven." Matthew 5:14-16 (KJV)

As a child of God, you are to let your light shine brightly so that others can see how great God is. Your life will inspire others to follow Christ as well. Being a leader is very important. As you follow Jesus, He molds you into a leader that others will follow. Your life should be an example of the way Christians ought to live. Let your light shine brightly, lighting the way for others to see their way more clearly on their own journeys.

Follow Jesus

—◆—

"And the people, when they knew it, followed Him: and He received them, and spake unto them of the Kingdom of God, and healed them that had need of healing." Luke 9:11 (KJV)

There will come a time in your life when you have to choose to stay in darkness or choose a path of light. Jesus heals all who follow Him, but that doesn't mean you won't stumble at times. It's better to be a follower of Christ who fails sometimes than one who fails to follow Jesus. Your failures are your learning experiences that come to help you grow. Your failures can be blessings if you choose to learn and grow from them.

FEBRUARY 17TH

Spirit of Gratitude

—◦◆◦—

"I will praise thee, O Lord, with my whole heart; I will shew forth all thy marvellous works." Psalm 9:1 (KJV)

It is so important to be grateful for everything God does in your life, no matter how big or small. Gratitude activates more. If God can see your gratitude in every situation, He will bless you with increase. He loves to bless His children with gifts, but if you can't be appreciative, why should He give you more? Show God that you can appreciate every blessing in your life, big or small. Watch your life change drastically. Make sure you always love the giver of the gift more than the gift.

Overpower Darkness

"And if one prevail against him, two shall withstand him; and a threefold cord is not quickly broken." Ecclesiastes 4:12 (KJV)

Satan will look for opportunities to slide in very smoothly if you're not careful. He will use people you love or strangers to distract you from what God is trying to do in your life. If someone comes up against you in an evil manner, use the light within you to overpower their darkness. Always stay in peace and love. When you let Jesus take control of the situation, the devil will flee. If two people stand in agreement, God will be in the midst of them. This creates a total of three and three cannot be easily broken. Overcome any kind of evil with the goodness God placed within you.

Opening Doors

—◆—

"I know thy works: behold, I have set before thee an open door, and no man can shut it: for thou hast a little strength, and hast kept My Word, and hast not denied My name." Revelations 3:8 (KJV)

God knows your heart. He sees everything. When you have faith in Him and do good deeds, He will open doors for you that no one can shut. In certain situations, it may be difficult for people to admit their faith in Christ for fear of what others may think or say. Do not deny Jesus no matter what or He will deny you before the Father. Keep His Word, remain faithful, and more doors will open for you.

FEBRUARY 20TH

Power over Satan

"Finally, brethren, whatsoever things are true, whatsoever things are honest, whatsoever things are just, whatsoever things are pure, whatsoever things are lovely, whatsoever things are of good report; if there be any virtue, and if there be any praise, think on these things." Philippians 4:8 (KJV)

Satan will put negative thoughts in your head and if you aren't careful, you will believe they're your own thoughts. Don't be deceived by Satan. If any negative thoughts enter your mind, don't entertain them. Cast them down the minute they enter your mind. If you think on positive things and fill your mind with good things, it's harder for Satan to put negative thoughts in your head. Use the power God gives to His children and take authority over the devil because he has no power. Whatever you feed your mind, will grow. Feed it positivity.

FEBRUARY 21ˢᵀ

Consuming Fire

———◆———

"Understand therefore this day, that the Lord thy God is He which goeth over before thee; as a consuming fire He shall destroy them, and He shall bring them down before thy face; so shalt thou drive them out, and destroy them quickly, as the Lord hath said unto thee." Deuteronomy 9:3 (KJV)

God will prepare things for you before you even get to certain areas of your life. When you follow Him, He will have blessings waiting for you when you arrive. He will destroy the enemy and bless you with the power to overcome your enemies very quickly. He will keep His promise to you. Just believe God and His Word. He has put His power within you because you are His child.

FEBRUARY 22ND

The Lord's Battle

———◆◆◆———

"The Lord shall fight for you; and ye shall hold your peace."
Exodus 14:14 (KJV)

God makes it clear that when trials and tribulations rise up, He will fight for you. Since you are His, nothing can stop His love for you and His fight over you. The Lord tells you that the battle is not yours, it's His. You need only to stand still. Pray constantly and keep your peace with everyone, even when they don't respect you in the same way you respect them. Pray for your enemies and God will take care of the rest. He will make sure you have victory as long as you remain in Him. God said He will never forsake His children and you need to remember that always. Continue to have faith in Him as He fights to bring you closer to your purpose.

Even-Tempered

———◦◦◦———

"He that hath knowledge spareth His words: and a man of understanding is of an excellent spirit." Proverbs 17:27 (KJV)

People will say and do things that are upsetting, but you have to use your knowledge in these situations by restraining your tongue. You are not going to like everyone you come across or everything people say to you, but stay in peace. Use self-control. As you gain an understanding of the Word, you will realize how important it is to stay even-tempered. Allow God to fight your battles. Remain in peace, hold your tongue, and pray for the person. As hard as this can be, it's very crucial for your well-being and it will change your life when you practice this. Always remember that no one can take your peace, you can only give it away.

Trample Satan

——◈——

"Behold, I give unto you power to tread on serpents and scorpions, and over all the power of the enemy: and nothing shall by means hurt you." Luke 10:19 (KJV)

As a child of God, you are blessed with the power to overcome any sin or darkness. It's important for you to realize your power as you come into the place God has called you to. The more you practice using your power and taking authority over the enemy, the stronger you become over your enemies. It becomes easier to identify demonic attack as you learn God's Word. Remain in God and nothing will defeat you. Use your power and trample the head of Satan. Remember that God wins in the end and as His children, we are victorious through Him.

FEBRUARY 25ᵀᴴ

Seek Good

❖

"He that diligently seeketh good procureth favour, but he that seeketh mischief, it shall come unto him." Proverbs 11:27 (KJV)

God highly favors those who do good works and good deeds for others. He will prosper you as He fills you with love, joy, peace, and happiness. The one who does evil will suffer evil. Everyone makes mistakes, but God knows your heart. He knows if you are a good person who happened to stumble or if you are filled with evil looking for trouble. Be careful for what you seek out because you just might find what you're looking for. Don't wait until it's too late to turn things around. You can start doing good today at this very moment.

FEBRUARY 26TH

Speak Life

"Let no corrupt communication proceed out of your mouth, but that which is good to the use of edifying, that it may minister grace unto the hearers." Ephesians 4:29 (KJV)

When you speak life and health to those around you, your words return back to you. Always encourage others by building them up. Words are so powerful. They can really pierce someone's soul. Make sure the words you speak will be beneficial to others because you will receive back what you give out. Speak love, life, and health to all God brings into your path.

True Friends

———✦◆✦———

"A man that hath friends must shew himself friendly: and there is a friend that sticketh closer than a brother." Proverbs 18:24 (KJV)

It's not everyday that you have friends that will stick by you through anything. You are blessed to have a friend that has your back no matter what. They will have your back, but will also be honest with you. They won't judge you, but they will help you if you fall. Be aware of people who call themselves friends, but are untrustworthy or unreliable. They may hurt you or cause you to stumble. Keep friends that are like brothers or sisters because these are the ones who will be there when no one else is. Be the kind of friend to others that you want them to be in return.

Shining on you

———◆———

"Wherefore He saith, 'Awake thou that sleepest, and arise from the dead, and Christ shall give thee light." Ephesians 5:14 (KJV)

You were dead in your sins before Christ met you in your dark place. Jesus met you in darkness to wake you up and give you light. You become more alive in Christ as you grow closer to Him. Don't go back into the wilderness and a life of sin, but continue to follow Jesus. Allow His light to shine on you and through you. Jesus guided you from darkness into His light and He blessed you with eternal life so that He could use you as a vessel to bring others into that same light.

The Lord's Discipline

———❖———

"My son, despise not the chastening of the Lord; neither be weary of His correction: For whom the Lord loveth He correcteth; even as a father the son in whom he delighteth." Proverbs 3:11-12 (KJV)

Our Heavenly Father is a father and a mother to those who don't have one. He will teach you lessons, but it's not to hurt you. He does it to grow you because He loves you and He wants you to be the best you can be. It would be worse if He ignored you and didn't care what you did. As a child of God, you won't get away with the same things others get away with because He disciplines those He loves. Always remember how blessed you are to have our Heavenly Father guiding you even when it hurts. No pain is wasted. All things are working together for your good.

Light of the Heart

———◆———

"For God, who commanded the light to shine out of darkness, hath shined in our hearts, to give the light of the knowledge of the glory of God in the face of Jesus Christ." 2 Corinthians 4:6 (KJV)

When you are in a dark place in your life, God will bring you out of it. The dark places are what helps you to grow. Darkness comes to remind you that you cannot do it on your own. When you've had enough heartache, lift your hands up and reach out to our Heavenly Father. When you truly accept Him into your heart, His light will guide your feet out of the dark place and your life will never be the same. Let His light shine brightly through you and around you. Darkness cannot overcome you.

God's Chosen People

———◆———

"Therefore, as God's chosen people, holy and dearly loved, clothe yourselves with compassion, kindness, humility, gentleness, and patience. Bear with each other and forgive one another if any of you has a grievance against someone. Forgive as the Lord forgave you. And over all these virtues put on love, which binds them all together in perfect unity." Colossians 3:12-14 (NIV)

We are God's chosen people. That is something so special that people who choose not to follow Christ can truly understand. It's our job as God's children to lead by example so others can see what life is like when you give your life to Jesus Christ. If someone hurts you, forgive them because God forgave you. Be a light to help someone else find their way out of pain and darkness.

Wait On The Lord

"And therefore will the Lord wait, that He may be gracious unto you, and therefore will He be exalted, that He have mercy upon you: for the Lord is a God of judgement: blessed are all they that wait for Him." Isaiah 30:18 (KJV)

Everyone comes to a point in their lives when they feel like they want to give up. They feel like they are forgotten. They feel hopeless and lose sight of their true purpose in life. BUT GOD, has a plan for all of us. You have to believe in something bigger than yourself. God will bless you with grace and mercy as He guides you toward your true calling in life. God has perfect timing. He knows exactly when to move you. When God tells you to move, don't hesitate. Follow His lead.

Working for the Lord

———◆———

"With good will doing service, as to the Lord, and not to men: Knowing that whatsoever good thing any man doeth, the same shall he receive of the Lord, whether he be bond or free." Ephesians 6:7-8 (KJV)

When God blesses you with an opportunity, put your all into it like you're doing it for Him and not people. Work hard in everything you do and God will reward you. Whenever you feel yourself getting tired, ask God to bless you with the strength and energy to accomplish the task. God will bring you into another level in your life once He sees that you can handle the level you're already on.

MARCH 6TH

Do Not Grumble

———◆———

"Do everything without grumbling or arguing, so that you may become blameless and pure, 'children of God without fault in a warped and crooked generation.' Then you will shine among them like stars in the sky as you hold firmly to the word of life. And then I will be able to boast on the day of Christ that I did not run or labor in vain." Philippians 2:14-16 (NIV)

Do not complain about things you have to do. Shine brightly as you work hard without a spirit of negativity or without grumbling. We are living in scary times. Everyone is all about themselves and what they can get, but don't be like them. Be the person God created you to be. Work with a spirit of positivity and love as your light brightens up the places God sent you to brighten up. We all have to give an account of what we've done here on earth. Make sure you are able to give an awesome account of your life and all the good work you've done.

Serve the People

"Only fear the Lord, and serve Him in truth with all your heart: for consider how great things He hath done for you." 1 *Samuel 12:24 (KJV)*

God will present you with opportunities to assist others that need help. This may include services such as financial, emotional, physical, mental, or spiritual assistance. When you're faithful to God, He will be faithful to your needs. Once He sees that He can trust you to serve Him and His children, He will provide for all of your needs. Continue serving God even when it feels like He isn't answering your prayers. It may feel that way sometimes, but He is testing your faithfulness. Are you serving God for stuff or out of love? Remain faithful to God through everything and He will bless whatever you do.

Incline your Heart

———◆———

"That He may incline our hearts unto Him, to walk in all His ways, and to keep His commandments, and His statutes, and His judgements, which He commanded our fathers." 1 Kings 8:58 (KJV)

God will go ahead of you to clear a path for your feet by devouring your enemies. He did the same thing for our ancestors. Turn your heart to our Heavenly Father and keep His ways. God is fair. He will not make you choose His way, but instead He blesses you with choices. You can choose to be a slave for Satan or you can choose to be a free child of God. Choose wisely because your choice will either keep you in bondage or free you.

Past Leaders

—◆—

"Remember them which have the rule over you, who have spoken unto you the word of God: whose faith follow, considering the end of their conversation." Hebrews 13:7 (KJV)

God sent us great leaders in the past who helped the people overcome all kinds of trials and tribulations in our country. Be more like them who were like Jesus Christ. Their faith in God is what transformed them into powerful leaders. If you follow God's direction for your life, one day you will look back over all the things the devil meant for evil and see how God used it for good. Your trials gave you more wisdom, strength, and power. You are more valuable in God's Kingdom now that you're discovering your true purpose in life. Choose to be a leader for God's people.

Build up Others

———◁◆▷———

"Wherefore comfort yourselves together, and edify one another, even as also ye do." 1 Thessalonians 5:11 (KJV)

When a bird is injured, a flock of birds will surround it to keep harm away from the bird. They protect the bird until it is able to regain its strength to fly again. We need to be the same way with one another, encouraging and nursing one another back to health. God loves to see His children come together as one because we are so much stronger together. Encourage as many people as you can today. We get a lot more accomplished when we're unified.

MARCH 11ᵀᴴ

God is Here

———◆———

"The Lord is nigh unto them that are of a broken heart; and saveth such as be of a contrite spirit." Psalm 34:18 (KJV)

We all go through painful situations in life, but how we deal with that pain is what matters most. When your heart is broken or your spirit is crushed, God is close by ready to comfort you and lift you up. Whenever you're hurting, do you lash out at others? Do you try to hurt yourself or those around you? You don't have to choose any of those options. You can reach out to our Heavenly Father for guidance. Don't be afraid to reach out to God. He is a loving Father. Trust Him to walk with you through any painful or uncomfortable situations.

MARCH 12TH

Use Your Hands

———◆———

"Let him that stole steal no more: but rather let him labour, working with his hands the thing which is good, that he may have to give to him that needeth." Ephesians 4:28 (KJV)

God is a loving and forgiving God. He will forgive those who have done wrong, including stealing. Once you are forgiven, stop stealing and start working with the hands you are blessed to have. Become an honest, hardworking citizen and help those who are in need. God will bless whatever you do. When you give to others, God will give it back to you more abundantly. Help others in need because you never know when you will need help.

Avoid Anger

———◆———

"Be not hasty in thy spirit to be angry: for anger resteth in the bosom of fools." Ecclesiastes 7:9 (KJV)

People are going to upset you sometimes. This seems to happen most often when you have a blessing coming your way. Satan will use people to take you out of your peace to devalue your blessing or to make you lose your blessing. It's important to remain patient with people and remain in peace. If you are right about a situation and you become angry trying to prove your point, then the enemy wins. Although you had a great point, your anger now makes you look wrong. Do not let anyone take your peace and remember that the Lord will fight your battles for you.

MARCH 14ᵀᴴ

The Lord's Reward

———◆———

"May the Lord repay you for what you have done. May you be richly rewarded by the Lord, under whose wings you have come to take refuge." Ruth 2:12 (NIV)

God will reward you for all the good you are doing. Continue to stay close to Him and allow Him to guide you. Trust God and remain faithful in your walk with Him. God will continue to protect you underneath His wings. Although the enemy will attempt to take you down, God will not allow any harm to come to you as you follow His lead. Do what the Lord asks of you and He will take great care of you.

Wait on the Lord

---◆---

"Rest in the Lord, and wait patiently for Him: fret not thyself because of him who prospereth in his way, because of the man that bringeth wicked devices to pass." Psalm 37:7 (KJV)

God will bring you into prosperity in your life when you continue to be patient and wait on Him to prosper you. Do not follow the example of others who look like they're succeeding, but are risking their salvation to prosper in wicked ways. It's none of your business what other people are doing to come into prosperity. The wicked will have to suffer the consequences of their actions when God decides to punish them. Remain focused on what God is doing in your life and not someone else's life. Stay in peace and learn to be happy for others when God blesses them. If you can be happy for others who are blessed, God will pour out His blessings over you.

Jesus Conquered Death

———◆———

"Forasmuch then as the children are partakers of flesh and blood, He also Himself likewise took part of the same; that through death He might destroy him that had the power of death, that is, the devil; And deliver them through fear of death were all their lifetime subject to bondage." Hebrews 2:14-15 (KJV)

Jesus is God in the flesh. He came so that you can have eternal life, free from death. You can enjoy life to the fullest when you have freedom, living without fear of where you're going when you die. Don't be afraid of anything and go wherever Jesus takes you. Live your life boldly and free in Christ. Don't be afraid to go out and explore different options until you find your true calling. God is with you through every step you take.

Ask for Anything

———⬧———

"This is the confidence we have in approaching God: that if we ask anything according to His will, He hears us. And if we know that He hears us - whatever we ask - we know that we have what we asked of Him." 1 John 5:14-15 (NIV)

God answers the prayers of a righteous person. When you pray to Him, believe that you have already received it. God can hear you and He is waiting to answer your prayers. Be confident when coming to our Heavenly Father. He is a Great Father. He loves to bless you and to make you smile. Always pray with confidence, remembering that God will never break His promises to you. Pray to God believing that the blessing is already yours.

Enjoy Life

"So I commend the enjoyment of life, because there is nothing better for a person under the sun than to eat and drink and be glad. Then joy will accompany them in their toil all the days of the life God has given them under the sun." Ecclesiastes 8:15 (NIV)

God expects you to do your part on this earth. You were made for a specific purpose. God created you to accomplish His work. Go out and work hard for the Lord wherever He places you. Remember that God put you wherever you are at this moment to make a difference. Enjoy every moment God blesses you with. Although you are expected to work hard, God wants you to also have joy. Live your life to the fullest because you only get one so make awesome memories for you and your loved ones.

Truth is Freedom

———◆———

"Then Jesus said to those Jews who believed Him, 'If you abide in My word, you are My disciples indeed. And you shall know the truth, and the truth shall make you free." John 8:31-32 (KJV)

When you follow Jesus, your faith grows more and more as you stay close to Him keeping His commandments. Jesus is your teacher so pay attention to all He is teaching you. He will reveal more and more truth to you as you follow Him. He will bless you with more wisdom, knowledge, and understanding as time goes on. His truth sets you free from Satan. God's truth opens your eyes allowing you to see what you were created to do on this earth. Learn God's truth and your life will change forever. You will learn to let go of things you cannot change and just be. Remain in perfect peace.

Be on Guard

————◆————

"Watch ye; stand fast in the faith, quit you like men, be strong. Let all your things be done with charity." 1 Corinthians 16:13-14 (KJV)

Always keep your eyes open and pray for discernment. Protect yourself from any kind of evil or darkness that may rise up against. Stand firmly in faith and always remain faithful to God. Be courageous, bold, and confident through our Heavenly Father. Allow Christ to be strong in your weakness. Remember to always do everything with a spirit of love.

Confessing Sins

—◆—

"Whoever conceals their sins does not prosper, but the one who confesses and renounces them finds mercy." Proverbs 28:13 (NIV)

There comes a time in our lives where we start to feel empty. The old things in our lives no longer feel satisfying to us and can no longer take us any further in life. This is the crossroads we all experience. We can either lay down and quit or we can choose to grow from our mistakes. The most powerful step to moving on from the past is to first admit your sins. God is very merciful. He will pour out His grace over you. Once you take that first step, you can no longer engage in those old behaviors. There is strength in admitting your downfalls. Be brave and confess your sins to God so He can forgive you. Then God can grow you into the person He created you to be.

Overflowing Hope

———⋙◈⋘———

"May the God of hope fill you with all joy and peace as you trust in Him, so that you may overflow with hope by the power of the Holy Spirit." Romans 15:13 (NIV)

Our Heavenly Father is a God of hope. As you trust Him completely in your life, He will fill you with joy which will strengthen you to do anything. Your peace will grow as you come to an understanding that no matter how bad things look, God won't bring you to anything He doesn't give you the power to withstand. You just have to trust Him. His Holy Spirit will overflow you with hope when you keep your mind focused on Him and not on the situation you're in. Ask yourself, "Am I truly trusting God?" Work on building up your faith in Him everyday.

Godly Sorrow

——◄►◆◄►——

"Godly sorrow brings repentance that leads to salvation and leaves no regret, but worldly sorrow brings death." 2 Corinthians 7:10 (NIV)

Everyone feels down at some point in their lives and that's alright because we're human. There is a difference in the kind of sorrows you may experience. Godly sorrow leads to repentance. Confess your sins to God and ask Him for forgiveness. He will bring you out of your sorrow and out of spiritual darkness. Once you call out to God, He will save you from eternal death. Worldly sorrow can lead you to death. It brings you into a dark place which can lead to depression or suicide. Always remember that you are not alone. Reach out to God and to the people who love you whenever you're feeling any kind of sadness. God will put His angels are all around you.

We See Light

"How priceless is Your unfailing love, O God! People take refuge in the shadow of Your wings. They feast on the abundance of Your house; You give them drink from Your river of delights. For with You is the fountain of life; in Your light we see light." Psalm 36:7-9 (NIV)

God's love is limitless and free. He protects you from the wicked schemes of the enemy by keeping you covered underneath His wings. God will make it so that you are never hungry or thirsty. He overflows you with an abundance of blessings because you are His and He delights in you. He breathed life into you when you were dead in your sins. Life flowed from within Him into you. God is the One and Only true light. Remain in His light and you will never be lost in darkness again.

Gladness

———◆———

"Then young women will dance and be glad, young men and old as well. I will turn their mourning into gladness; I will give them comfort and joy instead of sorrow." Jeremiah 31:13 (NIV)

Whenever you are tired of hurting and feeling sorrow, reach out to God. He is right there waiting for you to open your heart to Him. Once you turn toward God, He will comfort you through your mourning and replace your sorrow with His joy. You will still go through hardships, but you will be stronger through it because of His joy which will strengthen you. Let God's joy and comfort replace your sorrow. When Jesus returns, these are the things He will do for those who love Him. He will wipe away every tear you cry. Then He will fill you with His perfect peace and joy.

Test the Spirits

"Beloved, do not believe every spirit, but test the spirits, whether they are of God; because many false prophets have gone out into the world." 1 John 4:1 (NKJV)

Do not let anyone deceive you and turn you around. Continue to follow the teachings of Jesus Christ. People are going to come and speak into your life, but don't trust every person who claims to be of God. Satan also knows God's Word. You have to be aware of false doctrine. It's important to learn the Word and to know the real truth so that no one can deceive you. Remain in the Father and He will protect you from spirits that are not of Him. Be thankful to our Heavenly Father.

Stand Firm

"Be alert and of a sober mind. Your enemy the devil prowls around like a roaring lion looking for someone to devour. Resist him, standing firm in faith, because you know that the family of believers throughout the world is undergoing the same kind of sufferings." 1 Peter 5:8-9 (NIV)

Once you decide to follow Christ, the devil will try different ways to access you if you aren't careful. Resist anyone or anything that is not of the Lord. God will send His Holy Angels to protect you, but you still have to stay alert of who is coming into your presence. Attacks from the devil will make you stronger and will teach you to be more aware. All of God's children are experiencing the same kind of sufferings and attacks. This is why we ought to pray constantly for one another.

We Are Heirs

———⟫◆⟪———

"What, then, shall we say in response to these things? If God is for us, who can be against us? He who did not spare His own Son, but gave Him up for us all - how will He not also, along with Him, graciously give us all things?" Romans 8:31-32 (NIV)

As God's child, there is nothing in this world that can come up against you and win. God sacrificed His only Son so that you can have a relationship with Him and have eternal life. Our Heavenly Father made you an heir with Jesus. You received freedom and salvation the moment you decided to accept Christ into your heart. God chose to share His Kingdom with you. Show your gratitude to Him by allowing Him to use you as a vessel to strengthen and grow His Kingdom.

Avoid Bitterness

———◆———

"Get rid of all bitterness, rage and anger, brawling and slander, along with every form of malice. Be kind and compassionate to one another, forgiving each other, just as in Christ God forgave you." Ephesians 4:31-32 (NIV)

People will upset you or hurt you sometimes, but it's very important to avoid anger and falling into bitterness. If you allow someone to fill you with bitterness, you lose your power. They take your power the moment you become angry because anger takes you out of your character. Take your power back by forgiving others when they hurt. Remember that God also forgave you. If someone hurts you allow the Lord to fight your battles for you. He can take care of your enemies a lot better than you can. Things will turn out for the better when you let go and let God. Continue to be the loving, kind, and compassionate person God created you to be.

God's Handiwork

———❖———

"For we are God's handiwork, created in Christ Jesus to do good works, which God prepared in advance for us to do." Ephesians 2:10 (NIV)

God created you before you were born to do good works. He prepared you in advance for a special purpose. The more you learn about God the closer you will get to finding what your purpose is here on earth. It's exciting to learn what you were created to do. It's like an awesome adventure as you follow Christ toward your destiny. He has the key to your future so run after Him if you want to unlock it. Enjoy learning about the person God created you to be.

Don't Fear

———◆———

"Do not be afraid of those who kill the body but cannot kill the soul. Rather, be afraid of the One who can destroy both soul and body in hell." Matthew 10:28 (NIV)

The devil will attack you through people, but don't be afraid. Those people can only kill your flesh, but not your soul. Your soul will go wherever God decides to send it. The Bible tells you to be afraid only of the One who can destroy your body and soul in hell. "The One" refers to God. He is the One who can save you or dispose of you. Do not be discouraged by the devil and his attacks. Stay close to God and follow His ways because He is who decides where your soul will go when your flesh dies. Keep fighting the good fight.

Shine Your Light

"In the same way, let your light shine before others, that they may see your good deeds, and glorify your Father in Heaven."
Matthew 5:16 (NIV)

The longer you walk with God, the brighter the light within you shines. Continue to let your light shine brighter through your faithfulness to God allowing others to see your good works. When people who knew you before experience your transformation, they too will praise our Heavenly Father. As God's child, you want people to see the goodness God has filled you with because it leads to them also wanting a relationship with God. You were chosen by God to be a role model for others to follow. Allow others to see how much their life can change once they put God first in their own lives.

Fighting Temptation

———◄◆►———

"Because He Himself suffered when He was tempted, He is able to help those who are being tempted." Hebrews 2:18 (NIV)

Temptation is a natural part of life that everyone will experience at some point. It's not easy for anyone to deal with temptation, but Jesus can help you whenever you are being tempted. Jesus was also tempted by Satan a number of times, but He was able to overcome Satan. Jesus understands your struggle. He knows how you feel when you are tempted since He too was tempted by Satan. Jesus can help you overcome your own temptations, but you have to trust Him and reach out to Him for help. God always provides a way out, but it's your choice to take the way out. Keep a good clean support system around you. Stay close to people who are also following God's way.

Renewed Daily

———◆———

"Therefore we do not lose heart. Though outwardly we are wasting away, yet inwardly we are being renewed day by day. For our light and momentary troubles are achieving for us an eternal glory that far outweighs them all." 2 Corinthians 4:16-17 (NIV)

As you grow older, your body grows old too. Your body will waste away, but your inner man is being renewed daily and growing stronger. The troubles you face are going to hurt, but it's only temporary. Jesus is with you through all your troubles which will eventually pass. You are becoming stronger and wiser through every trial you overcome. Your troubles are preparing for you an eternal glory. None of the pain you've endured will be wasted. God uses all things to mold you into the person He created you to be. Don't quit before the change happens. Continue pressing on toward the mark. God is with you.

Christ Lives Within Me

———◦◦◦———

"I have been crucified with Christ and I no longer live, but Christ lives in me. The life I now live in the body, I live by faith in the Son of God, who loved me and gave Himself for me." Galatians 2:20 (NIV)

As you follow Christ, your old self will start to die. Jesus now lives through you. Sometimes you will suffer to follow Christ, but you will always be glorified with Christ as well. You will be blessed abundantly when you sacrifice and suffer for Christ. Keep your faith in Him through the good times and the bad times. Jesus laid down His life for you. He suffered to free you and to give you life even though He never sinned. Remember that everytime you feel like grumbling and complaining. Keep a spirit of love, humility, and gratitude.

A New Creation

———◆———

"Forget the former things; do not dwell on the past. See, I am doing a new thing! Now it springs up; do you not perceive it? I am making a way in the wilderness and streams in the wasteland." Isaiah 43:18-19 (NIV)

There isn't one person on this earth who doesn't have something in their past that they're not proud of. God tells us not to live in the past. When you begin following Christ, He will make you a brand new. He will wash away the old and bless you with the new. He leads you through the wilderness and He helps you find your purpose. It's a process to become who God created you to be. If you feel discouraged at any point along the way, don't quit no matter how tough things may get. Remember that the devil throws obstacles in your path, especially when you're going into the next level. Attacks from the devil means a promotion from God.

APRIL 6TH

Blessed Through Obedience

———◆———

"And all these blessings shall come on thee, and overtake thee, if thou shalt hearken unto the voice of the Lord thy God. Blessed shalt thou be in the city, and blessed shalt thou be in the field." Deuteronomy 28:2-3 (KJV)

Remain faithful to God through the good and the bad times. Stay obedient to God's Word. When you read God's Word, you learn His promises. Remember that no matter what's going on around you, God will never break His promises to you if you're loyal to Him. Your faith grows the more you trust Him and continue in His way even through the pain. If you practice self-discipline and self-control, God will rain down blessings over you that you won't have room enough to receive. He will bless you with more when He knows that He can trust you. He will bless wherever your feet walk and whatever your hands touch as He pours out His favor over you. Remain loyal to God and He will bless your life abundantly.

Practice What You Learn

"Those things, which ye have both learned, and received, and heard, and seen in me, do: and the God of peace shall be with you." Philippians 4:9 (KJV)

Remain in God's Word and keep His Word. Learn the truth Jesus Christ is teaching you and begin to practice it. You might fail sometimes, but don't give up. Those failures are chances to grow. Start to learn from your mistakes or you will be unhappy with yourself in this life. God's peace will stay with you as you get back up and try again. It is a process to master the current level you're on to get to the next level. Continue getting back up and have faith that God is leading you through to a new level.

Victory In Christ

"Now thanks be unto God, which always causeth us to triumph in Christ, and maketh manifest the savour of His knowledge by us in every place." 2 Corinthians 2:14 (KJV)

Always be grateful toward our Heavenly Father because He is who snatched you out of the hands of Satan. Christ leads you to freedom and victory. He saved you, cleaned you up, and set you apart for His use to bring others to His Heavenly Kingdom. God will pour out His Holy Spirit upon you blessing you with abundant life filled with love, joy, and peace. Stay close to God always.

APRIL 9TH

Prayer In Faith

"And the prayer offered in faith will make the sick person well; the Lord will raise them up. If they have sinned, they will be forgiven." James 5:15 (NIV)

Our Heavenly Father wants you to come to Him as you are. You don't have to wait until you're doing better to communicate with God. Jesus died for your sins. All you need to do is call out to Him and He will start to make you new. He will heal you mentally, physically, emotionally, and spiritually. Reach out to Him in faith. Your faith gives you access to His grace and mercy. He will heal any kind of sickness or hurt you're going through. Don't be afraid to call on our Heavenly Father because of your sins. God forgives all sin. Call out to Him in faith. He will show you the best way.

Glory In Tribulation

"And not only so, but we glory in tribulations also: knowing that tribulation worketh patience; And patience, experience; and experience, hope: And hope maketh not ashamed; because the love of God is shed abroad in our hearts by the Holy Ghost which is given unto us." Romans 5:3-5 (KJV)

Be glorified when trouble comes. God uses your troubles to help you grow in patience. He grows you into a stronger and wiser person. This produces hope as you strive to be the best version of yourself that you can be. The Holy Spirit has filled your heart with light and the love of God. Be still in the midst of trials because God is fighting for you. Your trials are strengthening you for what's coming next.

Standing On A Rock

———◆———

"He lifted me out of the slimy pit, out of the mud and mire; He set my feet on a rock and gave me a firm place to stand." Psalm 40:2 (NIV)

When you come into a dark place in your life, don't get discouraged. God will bring you out of any darkness into His light. Reach out to Him in faith. He will restore you and make your feet steady. Stand firmly like a rock when things are falling apart around you and remember that the storm will not last. This too shall pass. Trust God to turn your mess into a great message. Stand united together as one huge family in Christ and you will conquer anything the enemy throws your way.

APRIL 12ᵀᴴ

Reach Toward Your Destiny

"Brothers and sisters, I do not consider myself yet to have taken hold of it. But one thing I do: Forgetting what is behind and straining toward what is ahead, I press on toward the goal to win the prize for which God has called me heavenward in Christ Jesus." Philippians 3:13-14 (NIV)

It takes hard work to achieve your goals and to reach your destiny. But with God, all things are possible. Do not overwhelm yourself with trying to do everything perfectly. Take things step by step. Your first step is to let go of the past. Learn what you need to learn from your past and give it to God. Then one day at a time, one step at a time, walk in confidence to become the person God put you on this earth to be. Reach the destiny God has predestined for your life. You have more within you than you realize. As you walk hand in hand with God, He will slowly pull out all He placed within you.

God Chose Me

———◆◆◆———

"You did not choose Me, but I chose you and appointed you so that you might go and bear fruit - fruit that will last - and so that whatever you ask in My name the Father will give you."
John 15:16 (NIV)

Jesus makes it clear that He chose you. The troubles you go through will not be wasted. It hurts at the time you are going through your trials, but God will bring you out stronger than you were with a testimony to help someone else conquer their battle. He uses those He appointed to go and produce good fruit that will last. Our Heavenly Father will bless you with whatever you ask in the name of Jesus to help you accomplish His good and perfect will. Be grateful to be chosen by the Father.

APRIL 14TH

Jesus Was A Servant

———◆———

"For even the Son of Man came not to be ministered unto, but to minister, and to give His life a ransom for many." Mark 10:45 (KJV)

God sent His only begotten Son, Jesus, to die for you. Before He gave His life, He showed us all how we should live our lives here on earth. He was a great King among many, but He was very humble. He was a great King, but He became a servant to many. He cared about the needs of people and did all He could to meet those needs. Although He is God's Son, even He humbled Himself to be of service to those around Him, so shouldn't you? Don't be selfish. Find a way to be of service to someone else. Bring a little light or joy into someone's life today.

Prepared By God

———◆———

"When you pass through the waters, I will be with you; and when you pass through the rivers, they will not sweep over you. When you walk through the fire, you will not be burned; the flames will not set you ablaze." Isaiah 43:2 (NIV)

God will bring you into things that may feel pretty scary. It can be overwhelming, but if God brings you into something it's because He has already equipped you for it. Believe in yourself and trust in God. He will not let you be swallowed up or be overtaken by anything. Have faith in the One who created you. Know that God has prepared you and raised you up for a time such as this. Use the tools and the power God has placed within you.

Home With The Lord

"We are confident, I say, and would prefer to be away from the body and at home with the Lord." 2 Corinthians 5:8 (NIV)

Death of a loved one is not always easy to deal with. We love our friends and family so much that we never want to imagine them ever dying. We will all die one day. It's apart of life. When you learn more about Jesus and the spiritual realm, you start to understand that death in the physical world is actually the beginning to an everlasting life in the spiritual world. Your loved ones are in a better place than you are. They are home with the Lord and cheering you on every step of the way as you continue on your journey to your real home, Heaven. Enjoy life here and make the most of your human experience knowing that once you die, you will be reunited with your loved ones again.

APRIL 17ᵀᴴ

Show Me The Way

———◆———

"Let the morning bring me word of Your unfailing love, for I have put my trust in You. Show me the way I should go, for to You I entrust my life." Psalm 143:8 (NIV)

When you wake up in the morning, it's a good idea to pray to our Heavenly Father. Ask Him for His guidance. Trust God to lead you and guide you in your life. If you let Him lead the way, He will light up your path. He will remove any obstacles or stumbling blocks out of your way. When you ask Him for His guidance, be willing to listen because it won't always feel the way you expected it to feel. Always remember that God's way will always be the best way. All things will work together if it is God's will that you are following and not your own.

APRIL 18TH

Complete Trust In God

———◆———

"They will have no fear of bad news; their hearts are steadfast, trusting in the Lord." Psalm 112:7 (NIV)

As a child of God, you learn more and more to be fearless when it comes to new levels because you begin to trust in Jesus completely. You know that our Heavenly Father will never leave you to do anything alone. That doesn't mean bad or painful things will never happen, but you will feel God with you every step of the way as you continue on your path in the light. Trust God in the good times and definitely in the bad times. He is making your feet steady, allowing you to run on top of all things. Keep your faith in Him.

108

Your Labor Is Not In Vain

———◆———

"Therefore, my dear brothers and sisters, stand firm. Let nothing move you. Always give yourselves fully to the work of the Lord, because you know that your labor in the Lord is not in vain." 1 Corinthians 15:58 (NIV)

Do not let anything or anyone deceive you. Stand strong in what you believe. God brings people into your life, but Satan does too. Pay attention to who is around you and pray for discernment. Let the Lord use your hands to do good works in this evil world no matter how difficult it may get. Your work is not for nothing. The Lord will reward you for all you do. Continue trusting the Lord to pour out His favor over you as He blesses every sacrifice you make for the growth of His Kingdom.

Life In Jesus

―――◆―――

"We are afflicted in every way, but not crushed; perplexed, but not driven to despair; persecuted, but not forsaken; struck down, but not destroyed; always carrying in the body the death of Jesus, so that the life of Jesus may also be manifested in our bodies." 2 Corinthians 4:8-10 (ESV)

You will experience tough times, but they will not take you out. You may feel a little confused about what's going on in your life and wonder why you are going through it, but you are not left alone to do it on your own. You suffer at times, but you are made even stronger and wiser after after overcoming any trials you face. Always remember and be grateful for the sacrifice Jesus made so that you can live a full life. Thank You Jesus.

Faith And Thankfulness

———◆———

"So then, just as you received Christ Jesus as Lord, continue to live your lives in Him, rooted and built up in Him, strengthened in the faith as you were taught, and overflowing with thankfulness." Colossians 2:6-7 (NIV)

After you receive Christ into your heart, it's crucial to remain in Him. When you are grounded in Christ, your faith will grow as you see how drastically your life changes. You will overflow with peace, joy, and gratitude as you stay close to Jesus. Give yourself a break from the stress of doing things on your own separate from God. God is filling you with His strength. He wants to use you as a vessel and do great works through you. Allow Him to fill you with His Spirit as He strengthens you and blesses you to do all He has called you to do.

The Lord's Battle

***

"The Lord will fight for you; you need only to be still."
Exodus 14:14 (NIV)

When the devil comes in and tries to destroy you, Jesus will fight your battles for you. He will not let anyone or anything have victory over you even when things feel difficult. He will always work it out and have something or someone there to help you through any situation. When things are tough, keep repeating to God, "I trust You." He will not break His promise to you. He will not forsake His children. Remain calm whenever you feel like everything is falling apart. Remember that God will fight every battle you face, but you have to step back and let Him.

The Lord's Purpose Prevails

"Many are the plans in a person's heart, but it is the Lord's purpose that prevails." Proverbs 19:21 (NIV)

You as a human being may have many plans and ideas that you come up with. You become distracted from focusing on what God's plan for you is because of all these different ideas competing in your mind as you are trying to find your purpose. As hard as it can be, you need to be still and have patience. The Lord will move you when He is ready to move you. We cannot make God move when we think He should move. Stay faithful to Him and trust that He is moving behind the scenes to bring you into your purpose. It's simple, either you trust God or you don't. Do not give up hope because God is all powerful and what He says goes. He didn't forget about you. Trust Him.

God Doesn't Tempt Us

———◦◆◦———

"When tempted, no one should say, 'God is tempting me.' For God cannot be tempted by evil, nor does He tempt anyone; but each person is tempted when they are dragged away by their own evil desire and enticed." James 1:13-14 (NIV)

God will not tempt His children. It is Satan who tempts you and you can either fall into temptation or ask God to help you stand strong against temptations. Satan does not use new tricks. He uses the same tricks over and over because he knows that you are weak as a human being. You will fall for the same things every time if you don't do something about it. It's not easy, but with God's help, you can overcome anything Satan throws your way. Ask God to help you and He will always provide a way out of temptation.

God's Powerful Spirit

"For the Spirit God gave us does not make us timid, but gives us power, love, and self-discipline." 2 Timothy 1:7 (NIV)

When you are being guided by the Holy Spirit, you become less shy and more bold. You gain power through Jesus to do His will and not your own will. Your love for others grow a lot stronger giving you the kindness and compassion to help others in their situations. You gain self-control and self-discipline in your life which enables you to do what God is calling you to do. God will bless you with a sound mind and perfect peace as He guides you to new levels. Allow God to lead the way and guide you through whatever He has led you to. He will never let you down so trust Him completely.

Your Reward Is In Heaven

———⋄———

"Rejoice and be exceedingly glad, for great is your reward in Heaven, for so they persecuted the prophets who were before you." Matthew 5:12 (NKJV)

Before we were born, there were prophets persecuted. Jesus was persecuted and He suffered for all of us. This should give you more confidence to follow Jesus no matter how much you suffer to follow Him. You know that you will suffer at times, but you will also be glorified with Jesus. Rejoice and be glad because you know that God has your reward waiting for you in Heaven. Keep reaching toward God as He blesses you with great rewards for being a faithful servant.

God Armed You

———————

"You armed me with strength for battle; You humbled my adversaries before me." Psalm 18:39 (NIV)

Our Heavenly Father will not leave you or let anyone destroy you. He will prepare you and strengthen you for any battle you face. Be still and know that God will not let your enemies have victory over you. Remember to remain in God and allow Him to fight for you. You don't have to fear anything or anyone because you are covered by the blood of Christ. Your enemies will come for you, but God will continue to humble them and protect you. Let God fight your battles and bless you with victory.

Overcoming The Enemy

"You, dear children, are from God and have overcome them, because the One who is in you is greater than the one who is in the world." 1 John 4:4 (NIV)

When you are a child of God, His Holy Spirit lives within you. He gives you the power to overcome any obstacles that may come to make you stumble. He is greater than the one who is in the world. Satan is the ruler of this world, but God is greater than him, anything, or anyone. If you ever feel like giving up, keep going because the One who lives within you is all powerful and can conquer anything. By faith you will rise above and soar over any obstacle or trap the devil has set before you. Pay attention, stay focused, and stay prayed up.

Spirit of Servitude

———⟢◆⟣———

"Though I am free and belong to no one, I have made myself a slave to everyone, to win as many as possible." *1 Corinthians 9:19 (NIV)*

When you accept Jesus into your heart, He makes you free from the enemy. Although you are free, you must continue to serve the people around you. You make yourself a servant and relatable to whoever God puts in your path in order to win their soul over to Christ. You become God's hands, letting Him use you as a vessel to bring others to Him. None of us know the exact day or hour Jesus is coming back so it's important that we do our part to save as many souls as possible before it's too late. Do God's work and He will always do your work.

Christ's Triumphal Procession

"But thanks be to God, who always leads us as captives in Christ's triumphal procession and uses us to spread the aroma of the knowledge of Him everywhere." 2 Corinthians 2:14 (NIV)

Overflowing with gratitude toward God, praise Him because you are no longer in bondage. You were captives under the influence of Satan, but God led you out of captivity into victory through Jesus Christ. Now that you have escaped the darkness, you've entered into the light of Christ. He can now use you to spread the knowledge of Him everywhere and anywhere you go in order to bring others into His wonderful light. Let Jesus shine His light through you and around you helping others to see so they too can find their way out of darkness.

Divine Weapons

———⟢⬥⟣———

"For though we live in the world, we do not wage war as the world does. The weapons we fight with are not the weapons of the world. On the contrary, they have divine power to demolish strongholds. We demolish arguments and every pretension that sets itself up against the knowledge of God, and we take captive every thought to make it obedient to Christ." 2 Corinthians 10:3-5 (NIV)

God's children learn how to fight in the spiritual realm. We don't use the same fleshy weapons the world uses. We use divine weapons such as God's Word, guidance from the Holy Spirit, prayer, faith, hope, and love. These mighty weapons have the divine power you need to breakdown human pride, imaginations that sets itself up against God, strongholds, and walls. Fight your battles with God's divine power and no weapon formed against you shall prosper.

Protective Hedge

—◆—

"Have you not put a hedge around him and his household and everything he has? You have blessed the work of his hands, so that his flocks and herds are spread throughout the land." Job 1:10 (NIV)

God puts a hedge of protection around His children, their households, and everything they have. The enemy will try to come in and attack all you have, which is why it's so important to avoid falling into sin. Once you engage with the enemy, you create an opening for demonic attack. Continue praying constantly and communicating with our Heavenly Father. He will bless the work of your hands and allow you to reach others in order to help them. That's what the enemy is trying to stop, but don't allow that. You are stronger than his attacks because you are a child of the Most High. He gave you authority over the enemy so use your power.

Richly Rewarded

"May the Lord repay you for what you have done. May you be richly rewarded by the Lord, the God of Israel, under whose wings you have come to take refuge." Ruth 2:12 (NIV)

God will equip you with everything you need to accomplish any task He leads you to. The Lord will bless what you do and repay you for doing His work. He will always provide everything you need at the perfect time. He loves to reward His children for doing good deeds and following His path to righteousness. He is the One who keeps you protected underneath His wings. Show God your appreciation for all He does for you by helping someone else today.

Loving God and Others

———◆———

"Jesus said unto him, 'Thou shalt love the Lord thy God with all thy heart, and with all thy soul, and with all thy mind. This is the first and great commandment. And the second is like unto it, Thou shalt love thy neighbor as thyself." Matthew 22:37-39 (KJV)

When you put God first in your life, loving Him with all your might, He will guide your feet. He will walk with you through anything and everything. You will never be left to do anything alone. He is right there waiting to catch you before you fall. The second thing Jesus tells you to do, is love others as you love yourself. If you keep our Heavenly Father at the center of your life, the love He pours out over you will overflow into the lives of those around you. Love others through the good times and the hard times the way God loves you.

Have Faith

———⊰◆⊱———

"He said to His disciples, 'Why are you so afraid? Do you still have no faith?" Mark 4:40 (NIV)

Fear and worry can creep up in your mind even when you are walking with God. They can keep you up at night if you let them. Replace your fears and worries with gratitude toward God. If you notice any fear or doubt creeping up, keep telling God thank you for all He has already done in your life. Sometimes your faith is tested. Will you continue to be worried or have genuine faith that God is bigger than any problem you are facing right now? God has the final say on everything. Keep going forward even when fear is there. That is true courage and real faith.

The Battle Isn't Yours

———◆◆◆———

"Do not repay anyone evil for evil. Be careful to do what is right in the eyes of everyone. If it is possible, as far as it depends on you, live at peace with everyone. Do not take revenge, my dear friends, but leave room for God's wrath, for it is written: 'It is mine to avenge; I will repay,' says the Lord. On the contrary: 'If your enemy is hungry, feed him; if he is thirsty, give him something to drink. In doing this, you will heap burning coals on his head.' Do not be overcome by evil, but overcome evil with good." Romans 12:17-21 (NIV)

Remain in peace with everyone, no matter how they may treat you. God defends you from people who don't have your best interest at heart. Stop wasting energy fighting those who don't like you for no reason at all. Avoid falling into anger which causes bitterness. God fights for all of His children. Remember to stay in peace throughout the day and allow God to fight for you.

Live as a Believer Everywhere

———◆———

"Nevertheless, each person should live as a believer in whatever situation the Lord has assigned to them, just as God has called them. This is the rule I lay down in all the churches."
1 Corinthians 7:17 (NIV)

God doesn't make you answer His call. When He calls you, remember how blessed you are. When He places you somewhere, don't hesitate to do what He has assigned you to do. Wherever you are led by the Lord, make sure you use the power He has filled you with and affect the atmosphere. You are the one He has anointed for the job. He has you in that place for a reason. Bring greatness into the room whenever you are inside of it. Be the change you want to see and lead others with a spirit of positivity. Things will flow so much better whenever you and the people around you have a spirit of unity. Let God shine and be seen in your work.

God Uses Your Hurt

———◦◆◦———

"You intended to harm me, but God intended it for good to accomplish what is now being done, the saving of many lives."
Genesis 50:20 (NIV)

People will hurt you sometimes and although it's hard to understand why, God will use what hurt you to help others. The devil will try to destroy you through people or through things. When the pain gets bad enough you will eventually turn to God for help. He will pick you up and make you a new person. He will take the same thing the devil used to harm you and use it for your good. He will use it for the good of others. Once you are saved and transformed through Jesus, you receive God's seal of approval to bring others to Him. He is using you to save many lives. Don't be afraid to tell your testimony to others because you never know whose life you might save.

Heirs with Jesus

"Because you are His sons, God sent the Spirit of His Son into our hearts, the Spirit who calls out, 'Abba, Father.' So you are no longer a slave, but God's child; and since you are His child, God has made you also an heir." Galatians 4:6-7 (NIV)

God sent His Son, Jesus, to die for us all. Once you decide to accept Christ, He lives within you. Now you are free and you are adopted into God's family as His very own child. As a child of the Most High, you are heirs with Christ and are given anything you ask for in Jesus' name according to His will. You will live in eternity with our Heavenly Father and receive the Kingdom of Heaven. Remind yourself that the troubles you face today are temporary and encourage yourself with His Word. We are kings and queens through Christ, so live as one.

Lord, You Know Me

"You have searched me, Lord, and You know me. You know when I sit and when I rise; You perceive my thoughts from afar. You discern my going out and my lying down; You are familiar with all my ways." Psalm 139:1-3 (NIV)

God created you. He knows everything about you. You can't hide anything from Him. He knows every thought you have before you even think it. There is no reason to try and hide from God because you can't. Instead of pretending you're something you're not, ask God to make you the person He created you to be. It feels good to have a genuine spirit, a spirit of truth. Once God begins to shape you into who He meant for you to be, you won't feel any shame or care what anyone else thinks. Be free to live for God and not for others. Find your true purpose through our Heavenly Father and soar into your destiny.

Reliance On God

———◆◆◆———

"We do not want you to be uninformed, brothers and sisters, about the troubles we experienced in the province of Asia. We were under great pressure, far beyond our ability to endure, so that we despaired of life itself. Indeed, we felt we had received the sentence of death. But this happened that we might not rely on ourselves, but on God, who raises the dead." 2 Corinthians 1:8-9 (NIV)

Following Jesus, changes your life for the better. You become a new creation, but you still have troubles. You learn how to deal with trouble in a healthier way. You can still have peace in the midst of any storm, remembering that all things work together. Certain situations can be painful, but it reminds you to depend on God in everything. Pain keeps you humble and teaches you to stay close to God. It keeps you from straying too far off the path. You have the same power within you that God uses to raise the dead. You have nothing or no one to fear.

Walking In The Spirit

"If we live in the Spirit, let us also walk in the Spirit. Let us not be desirous of vain glory, provoking one another, envying one another." Galatians 5:25-26 (KJV)

It's important to stay in the Spirit. It's not always easy, but whenever you feel yourself slipping away from God's will, pray to Him. Get yourself centered again through Jesus. When you are walking with Jesus, you become glorified through Him. You receive great blessings, but make sure you aren't bragging about them to provoke others. Do not envy others either. Learn to be happy for others when they are blessed and God will bless you in His perfect timing.

Don't Judge Anyone

———◆———

"There is only one Lawgiver and Judge, the One who is able to save and destroy. But you - who are you to judge your neighbor?" James 4:12 (NIV)

God is the One who chooses to save or destroy. He made the law and He is also the Judge since He created all things. You are not able to save or to destroy souls because you are merely human beings. None of us are without sin, which means you don't have any right to judge what someone else is doing or what they've done. It's important to help others, but help them without judging what they are doing. You are to correct your neighbor if they are doing wrong, but do it in love to help them not to hurt them. God will put you in someone else's shoes when you judge them in order to teach you not to judge others. If you see your neighbor struggling, give them a hand in a spirit of love.

Strengthen Your Inner Being

———•◆•———

"I pray that out of His glorious riches He may strengthen you with power through His Spirit in your inner being, so that Christ may dwell in your hearts through faith." Ephesians 3:16-17 (NIV)

You will grow stronger in Christ through the power of His Holy Spirit. Your life becomes a life filled with blessings. From glory to glory, your faith grows as you learn to be grateful for everything God is doing in your life. Even through tribulations your faith and appreciation grows as your inner being is strengthened. Jesus dwells in your heart through faith and works through you. He changes the way you see your life. Your perspective on things will change which leads to a greater, happier, and more glorious life. Keep trusting in God and don't let anything deceive or discourage you from the real truth.

Under God's Mighty Hand

"Humble yourselves, therefore, under God's mighty hand, that He may lift you up in due time. Cast all your anxiety on Him because He cares for you." 1 Peter 5:6-7 (NIV)

Pain doesn't feel good to anyone. Your trials can be really tough to get through successfully, but with God all things are possible. The pain comes to remind you to depend on our Heavenly Father. It keeps you from falling into pride, remembering that apart from God you can do nothing. In God's perfect timing, He will exalt you. If you try to force things to happen too fast, you will overwhelm yourself and have to start all over again. Keep your eyes focused on God and He will walk with you through each step as He has ordered them. He will add everything you need as you follow Him. He loves you and He cares so much for you. Do you truly trust Him? If so, remain in perfect peace while resting in His loving arms, trusting Him to protect and guide you through it all.

God-Breathed Scripture

———◆———

"All Scripture is God-breathed and is useful for teaching, rebuking, correcting, and training in righteousness, so that the servant of God may be thoroughly equipped for every good work." 2 Timothy 3:16-17 (NIV)

It's important to read your Holy Bible and to study scripture so that you can be a great servant for the Lord. God breathed on the Word and it is now living water for our souls. It is crucial for God's beloved children. God God teaches, rebukes, and trains the righteous through this Life-Giving Book. Learn the Truth so you can follow it and be the best person you can be here on earth. If you want to live a more fulfilling life, don't wait another second to receive the best gift ever. Make sure you reserve your spot next to the King in Heaven. Nothing is more important than your focus on Jesus.

The Lord Is My Light

———◆———

"The Lord is my light and my salvation - whom shall I fear? The Lord is the stronghold of my life - of whom shall I be afraid? When the wicked advance against me to devour me, it is my enemies and my foes who will stumble and fall. Though an army besiege me, my heart will not fear; though war break out against me, even then I will be confident." Psalm 27:1-3 (NIV)

When you are God's child, there is nothing to fear. God is your protector. Whenever your enemies come up against you, they will fall. Sometimes the enemy will send a spiritual attack against you through people, but remain confident. You know God is mightier than anything or anyone. Always remember that God is your refuge and your help in times of trouble. If the enemy attacks you, call on God to fight your battles. Don't try to do it alone because you might fall. Stay close to God, He will protect you and give you victory.

God Hears Our Prayers

———◆———

"And if we know that He hears us - whatever we ask - we know that we have what we asked of Him." 1 John 5:15 (NIV)

God loves to bless His children. If you ask our Heavenly Father for anything and have faith that He will do it, He will give it to you. Pray constantly to God and know that He is always listening. He will answer your prayers according to His will for your life. Whenever you pray for something, believe you already have it and be patient. Wait for God's perfect timing. If you have true faith in God, you know that He hears you so don't get discouraged if you don't get what you asked for right away. He will answer your prayers at the right time.

Love and Encouragement

———

"And let us consider how we may spur one another on toward love and good deeds, not giving up meeting together, as some are in the habit of doing, but encouraging one another - and all the more as you see the Day approaching." Hebrews 10:24-25 (NIV)

God blesses you with certain people in your life. He wants you to love and encourage others. Do good deeds for other people. Relationships are very important to have. It's crucial to be there for others in their time of need. If you do this, God will bless you with good people in your time of need. None of us know the exact day or hour Jesus is coming. God's Word tells us to meet together and to encourage one another, especially as the Day is approaching. Jesus will be back and you have to be ready. Love and support each other. Be grateful to God for the people He's placed in your path to help you through good times and the tough times as He is perfecting you.

The Lord Is At Your Side

———◆———

"Have no fear of sudden disaster or of the ruin that overtakes the wicked, for the Lord will be at your side and will keep your foot from being snared." Proverbs 3:25-26 (NIV)

Walking with the Lord gives you comfort because you know that He will not let you fall. He will keep you from being trapped by the wicked or falling into ruin that overtakes them. The Lord never promised you that you wouldn't have trouble, but He will walk through it with you. He will not leave you to be overtaken by fear or evil. He will hold your hand and guide you through every battle that rises up against you. You can't control people or things, but you can ask God for help dealing with the stress they can bring. Don't be so quick to give up when the enemy attacks you. Fight even harder knowing that the Powerful Almighty God Himself is living within you to help you win the victory.

Seek God, Find Favor

"Whoever seeks good finds favor, but evil comes to one who searches for it." Proverbs 11:27 (NIV)

Do not become easily influenced by others to do evil. Continue to do good deeds and the Lord will give you favor. If you look for trouble, don't be surprised when you find it. You get whatever you give out. If you are looking to do evil, you bring evil upon yourself. You won't get far in life doing evil deeds. Let your goodness overcome the evil that comes against you. Let your light conquer any darkness that surrounds you. Jesus was also attacked, but He didn't let that change who He was. He remained in peace. Follow His example as you too conquer darkness.

Enduring Temptation

"Blessed is the man that endureth temptation: for when he is tried, he shall receive the crown of life, which the Lord hath promised to them that love Him." James 1:12 (KJV)

We all go through times of testing in our lives. The ones who are able to persevere in trials are considered blessed. Every new level in your life brings a new devil. None of us are able to avoid trouble because it builds character. God uses trials and tribulations to grow you into the person He destined you to be. There are certain characteristics that won't work for the new level you are on. It's time to let go of some of your old ways to persevere in this new life God is giving you a chance to have. If you can endure temptation, God promises you the crown of life if you love Him. Be strong and remember the trials you experience will pass.

God Fulfills His Promises

"God is not a man, that He should lie; neither the son of man, that He should repent: hath He said, and shall He not do it? Or hath He spoken, and shall He not make it good?"
Numbers 23:19 (KJV)

God is a Spirit of Truth. He cannot lie. Whatever God said on the matter settles it. He will not change His mind. God cannot break His own Word or promises. He is the Father of Truth. It's important to learn the promises of God and to learn about your inheritance in Christ. When you follow His teachings, you will understand all He has given you and all that is yours. Your faith will grow as you see the hand of God moving in your life. God will not fail you and He will fulfill every promise He has promised to those who love Him. Trust in His Word.

Love Others Deeply

———◆———

"Now that you have purified yourselves by obeying the truth so that you have sincere love for each other, love one another deeply, from the heart." 1 Peter 1:22 (NIV)

When God saves you from a sinful life, it's important to read His Word. Learn the truth and obey it. Don't only listen to the Word, but also do what it says to become purified children with a clean heart. God will overflow you with His love and it will overflow into the lives of those around you. Love the people that God puts in your path. His Word tells us to love one another deeply. We are considered children of light for a reason. God's light needs to shine brightly through us so that others can find their way out of darkness and into the path of light. Continue to love others unconditionally.

Get Acquainted With God

————◆————

"And such as do wickedly against the covenant shall He corrupt by flatteries: but the people that do know their God shall be strong, and do exploits." Daniel 11:32 (KJV)

Do not let wickedness take over you. Be careful about the people you let speak into your life. Do not be deceived. God uses people for good, but Satan also uses people for evil. He will corrupt your spirit with flattery through other people. The people who not only believe in God, but truly know their God shall be strong. He will do great exploits through those who know and love Him. Stay focused on God and His promises. Do not let Satan distract you from what God is doing in your life. Pray that God will give you the focus of a tiger and go after what God has given you to possess.

Delivered From Affliction

———◆———

"Many are the afflictions of the righteous, but the Lord delivereth him out of them all." Psalm 34:19 (KJV)

Following Jesus is not easy, but it's worth it. Although you are righteous, there will be trials along the way. There will be difficulties that you go through, but Jesus will deliver you from it all. You can't give up hope. Hold on tight to Him no matter how things are looking. God does not save you only to torture you later down the road. He saved you because He truly loves you. God will use what the devil meant for evil and use it for good. Trust in our Lord every step of the way as He holds your hand through it all. He will not let you stumble or fall. Keep your faith knowing that if God brought you to it then He will also bring you through it.

Your Faith Pleases God

———◆◆◆———

"And without faith it is impossible to please God, because anyone who comes to Him must believe that He exists and that He rewards those who earnestly seek Him." Hebrews 11:6 (NIV)

You have to first believe that God exists and then have faith in Him. You can't please God without faith. Your faith grows more and more as you follow Him. He will do many great things in your life and grow you into who He created you to be as you learn more about Him. You will look back on your life and realize that you are a new person with new ways. As God transforms you, He blesses you with perfect peace. Keep your eyes focused on God through everything. Our Heavenly Father will rain down blessings over your life and reward you as you continuously seek Him. His way is the best way so let Him guide you in all you do today.

Proclaim His Name

—◆—

"What I tell you in the dark, speak in the daylight; what is whispered in your ear, proclaim from the roofs. Do not be afraid of those who kill the body, but cannot kill the soul. Rather, be afraid of the One who can destroy both soul and body in Hell." Matthew 10:27-28 (NIV)

When you spend time with God alone, He teaches you through His Word. He blesses you with wisdom, knowledge, understanding, and revelation. He doesn't bless you just for you. He wants you to pass on what He teaches you to others. The more you give to others what He gives you, the more He will bless you. Don't be afraid to shout about Jesus to anyone. They cannot save or kill your soul. Your life here on earth is temporary, but your soul will spend an eternity in Heaven or Hell. If you can't tell others you belong to Jesus, He will not tell the Father you belong to Him. Let people know you are God's beloved child.

Made Alive In Jesus

"But because of His great love for us, God, who is rich in mercy, made us alive with Christ even when we were dead in transgressions - it is by grace you have been saved." Ephesians 2:4-5 (NIV)

We as human beings are evil by nature. We are sinful creatures, but because of the great love God has for His children, He sent His Son to die for our sins. None of us deserve anything, but God is rich in mercy. His grace is what saved us. Jesus was perfect and without sin, but He died for us so that we can be made alive in Him. We can't be good enough to earn favor with God. Once you receive Christ into your heart, you are saved from eternal death. We have victory through Jesus because He conquered death. Be grateful for the sacrifice Jesus made on the cross for you.

Prosperity Through Jesus

"For I know the plans I have for you," declares the Lord, "plans to prosper you and not to harm you, plans to give you hope and a future. Then you will call on Me and come and pray to Me, and I will listen to you. You will seek Me and find Me when you seek Me with all your heart." Jeremiah 29:11-13 (NIV)

God doesn't try to hurt you, but there is pain in the process of transformation. The process isn't always going to feel so great, but the end result is worth all the suffering you endure. God wants to grow you, give you hope, and a bright future. As He prospers you, He gives you permission to call on Him for anything. He says you can come to Him and He will listen. It is amazing He loves us this much. Seek Him wholeheartedly and you will find Him.

Clean Spirit

———◆———

"Wherefore lay apart all filthiness and superfluity of naughtiness, and receive with meekness the engrafted word, which is able to save your souls." James 1:21 (KJV)

God is a Spirit of Love and Goodness. It's very crucial to spend time with Him every morning before you start your day. Let Him help you rid yourself of any evil or filth. Rid yourself daily of pride by becoming humble and admitting that you need God's guidance in everything you do. When you humble yourself and follow Jesus, you will begin changing in ways you never thought possible. Fill yourself with God's Divine Word and let the power of His Word make you a new creation. God's Word is what will save you.

Submit To God

—◆—

"Acquaint now thyself with Him; and be at peace: thereby good shall come unto thee." Job 22:21 (KJV)

God is the only One who can bless you with prosperity. When you come to Him in humility and submit to His will, He guides you on an exciting journey. He blesses you with perfect peace as you remain in Him. You will experience storms in your life at times, but He will allow you to have perfect peace in those storms. When you are going through trials, He is right there with you. Acknowledge His presence and be grateful for His guidance. Pray to Him constantly and be courageous through Him. He will hold you and keep you from falling. God has a blessing waiting on you for every battle you win. Stay close to Him as He prospers you into greatness.

God Of All Grace

———◆———

"And the God of all grace, who called you to His eternal glory in Christ, after you have suffered a little while, will Himself restore you and make you strong, firm, and steadfast." 1 Peter 5:10 (NIV)

Everyone goes through a time of suffering before they come to God. Painful things happen in your life before you choose to walk with Him. After your suffering, God calls you to Him. He will strengthen you and restore you. He makes your feet steady and brings you into relationship with Him. He chose to bless you with victory. Be grateful to be a child of a King. You are royalty through Jesus Christ. Keep that in mind throughout your day.

We Aren't Judges

———◆◆◆———

"How can you say to your brother, 'Brother, let me take the speck out of your eye,' when you yourself fail to see the plank in your own eye? You hypocrite, first take the plank out of your own eye, and then you will see clearly to remove the speck from your brother's eye." Luke 6:42 (NIV)

None of us are perfect. Be careful from judging someone else when there are things you could fix yourself. Don't make others around you feel like they are bad especially since you also have imperfections. When you are correcting someone else, do it in love to help them grow into a better person. When you judge others, it only makes them want to run the other way. If you judge others, you will also be judged. Love one another by helping each other without any judgement.

God Over Everything

———◆———

"By faith Moses, when he had grown up, refused to be known as the son of Pharaoh's daughter. He chose to be mistreated along with the people of God rather than to enjoy the fleeting pleasures of sin. He regarded disgrace for the sake of Christ as of greater value than the treasures of Egypt, because he was looking ahead to his reward." Hebrews 11:24-26 (NIV)

When you sacrifice for God He will reward you. Don't let treasures be your god. Learn to wait on God to bring you into prosperity. Don't let the wicked entice you with prosperity because that will not last. Sacrifice and be patient, keeping in mind that God's reward is of greater value than the pleasures of this world. In God's perfect timing He will pour you out a blessing you won't have room enough to receive. Choose God over everything since He owns everything anyway.

Comforting Others

---◆---

"Praise be to the God and Father of our Lord Jesus Christ, the Father of compassion and the God of all comfort, who comforts us in all our troubles, so that we can comfort those in any trouble with the comfort we ourselves receive from God."
2 Corinthians 1:3-4 (NIV)

We all experience troubles in our lives, but God is an awesome Father and He comforts us in those times of trouble. He is very compassionate toward His children and He will send help through the Holy Spirit or through other people. You are His child and you are made in His image so strive to be more like Him. If there is a brother or sister in trouble, comfort them the same way our Heavenly Father comforts you. Be compassionate and understanding of what someone else may be going through. Be to someone else what you would want from others if you were in trouble. Spread love to whoever God places in your path.

JUNE 6ᵀᴴ

Do Not Be Moved

———◆———

"Therefore, my dear brothers and sisters, stand firm. Let nothing move you. Always give yourselves fully to the work of the Lord, because you know that your labor in the Lord is not in vain." 1 Corinthians 15:58 (NIV)

People will not always like you because of your faith in Jesus, but the Holy Bible tells us that we are blessed when we are persecuted for Jesus' name. Don't let anyone or anything stop you from speaking His name. Continue to do what He is leading and guiding you to do because He sees it. He will not let your work be done in vain. God is bigger than everything. With Him on your side, no one or nothing can come up against you. Shine brightly in the work you do for the Lord because He is with you and protecting you. He is the One in charge.

His Glory Is On You

—⟡—

"For, behold, the darkness shall cover the earth, and gross darkness the people: but the Lord shall arise upon thee, and His glory shall be seen upon thee." Isaiah 60:2 (KJV).

We are living in a world filled with darkness and pain. People are lost in darkness. They are like the walking dead, but God chose you to be a light to help others see. His glory is all over you for others to see how real and true He is. Let God use you as a vessel to bring good into a fallen world. We can't pretend that we don't see the world getting worse. We know that we don't have forever before the Lord comes back. Do not take a chance on waiting for your soul to be saved. If you are saved, use the gifts the Lord has given you to glorify Him and help save the souls of others. Be a light.

Eternal Glory

—◆—

"Therefore we do not lose heart. Though outwardly we are wasting away, yet inwardly we are being renewed day by day. For our light and momentary troubles are achieving for us an eternal glory that far outweighs them all." 2 Corinthians 4:16-17 (NIV)

Go forward with courage even when it hurts. Don't let any troubles stop you from rising. The troubles will pass and when it does, you will be stronger if you don't give up. You will be renewed daily as you put one foot in front of the other. It's important to keep moving and not quit. You will suffer at times following Christ, but the glory you will achieve is far more greater than what you suffered to stay faithful. First crawl, walk, run, and then soar into your destiny. You can do it!

The Word Of God

———◆———

"This is the meaning of the parable: The seed is the Word of God. Those along the path are the ones who hear, and then the devil comes and takes away the Word from their hearts, so that they may not believe and be saved." Luke 8:11-12 (NIV)

When you are following Jesus, you become a target. The devil will use people or things to come up against you and to steal what God put within your heart. Guard your heart and pay attention to who comes into your life. Don't allow anyone to deceive you and turn you away from the Truth. Keep the Word in your heart and continue to believe God's Word so that you will be saved when the Lord comes back for the righteous. Stand firm in the Word.

Worship In Spirit and Truth

———❦———

"Yet a time is coming and has now come when the true worshipers will worship the Father in the Spirit and in truth, for they are the kind of worshipers the Father seeks. God is Spirit, and His worshipers must worship in the Spirit and in truth." John 4:23-24 (NIV)

God chose you. It's important to grab a hold of Him. Don't let go. Keep your eyes focused on Him. God wants authentic believers who truly loves Him and trust Him every step of the way. Worship Him in truth and in Spirit because He is a Spirit. The closer you draw to God, the closer He will draw to you. He is transforming you. He wants you to focus on Him, ignoring all distractions. Walk with Him and just be, God will do the rest. Your light shines brighter when you relax.

Don't Lose Focus

---◆---

"Therefore I tell you, do not worry about your life, what you will eat or drink; or about your body, what you will wear. Is not life more than food, and the body more than clothes?"
Matthew 6:25 (NIV)

Satan likes to send distractions to take your mind off of God anyway he can. He will use people to distract you or attack you. He will use people you love to hurt you. He attacks your health, finances, or anything else of value. God tells you not to worry about anything. Keep your focus on Him. Your mind is the most powerful weapon you have, which is why Satan will use anything he can to take your peace of mind. If he can keep you stressed out from worrying and unmotivated, than he has done his job. Let God be your only goal today and He will add everything you need as you remain in Him.

There Is One Judge

———⟩◆⟨———

"The person with the Spirit makes judgements about all things, but such a person is not subject to merely human judgements, for, 'Who has known the mind of the Lord so as to instruct Him?' But we have the mind of Christ." 1 Corinthians 2:15-16 (NIV)

When you are a child of God, you have His Spirit living within you. He will give you direction and lead you. If you are not sure of what steps you should take next, look to Him for guidance. Don't look to unbelievers for spiritual advice. They don't understand the spiritual realm and may judge you because they are without spiritual understanding. Listen for instructions from the Holy Spirit as He is guiding you. Take instruction from the Lord because He is your Creator. Do not let the judgements of others turn you around from the purpose God has placed deep down inside of you.

Do Not Grumble

"Neither murmur ye, as some of them also murmured, and were destroyed of the destroyer." 1 Corinthians 10:10 (KJV)

It's very crucial to keep an attitude of gratitude throughout your life. It's not good to complain about everything because you miss out on what the Lord is trying to teach you or even when He is blessing you. The more grateful you are, the more God will bless you. When you grumble, it's hard for people to want to help you or be around you. It's hard for God to use you as a vessel to do good works when no one wants to even be wherever you are because of your ungrateful attitude. Don't let a negative attitude kill your spirit. Keep a positive, grateful, loving attitude and watch the Lord rain down blessings over you. Being grateful activates God to bless you with more.

God's Approval

"For do I now persuade men, or God? or do I seek to please men? For if I yet pleased men, I should not be the servant of Christ." Galatians 1:10 (KJV)

Walking with the Lord can be difficult sometimes. People who knew you before you were saved will look at you differently. They will say, "You've changed." Remember that it's actually a compliment when they say that to you. It's good to become a changed, new creature in Christ. Do not live your life trying to please other people because it's impossible anyway. You will hurt yourself trying to live up to everyone else's expectations. You are God's servant so be who He called you to be. You are free to be who God created you to be.

Jesus Is The Son

---◆---

"Jesus said to them, 'If God were your Father, you would love Me, for I have come here from God. I have not come on My own; God sent Me." John 8:42 (NIV)

God sent His only Son to this world as our Savior. Jesus let it be known that if you are truly God's child then you would love Him also. God sent Him to save you from your sins. If other people believe in different gods, it's not up to you to judge them. There is only one Judge. You have to love others no matter what their religion may be, but don't be swayed from your own beliefs in Jesus. Demonstrate the love of Jesus by loving others and your example may be just the thing someone else needed to see to spark their own love for Jesus. Live in peace with everyone and let God do the judging. Continue being a living example for what Christ has done in your life and can do in someone else's life.

You Are Forgiven

"Therefore, I tell you, her many sins have been forgiven - as her great love has shown. But whoever has been forgiven little loves little." Luke 7:47 (NIV)

We have a very merciful Father in Heaven. He is willing to forgive all sins. When you come to Him with a pure heart and ask Him for forgiveness, He will wash away your sins. He will pick you back up and help you find your way. The one who God forgives the most, loves the most because of their gratitude for a new beginning. It's hard not to be full of gratitude after God wipes your slate clean. He doesn't care what you've done in your life, He just wants you to come to Him. Depend on Him always and accept His love for you. He is waiting for you to completely surrender to Him. Don't be afraid to give your life to our Creator.

Follow Jesus Immediately

"And He said to them, "Follow Me, and I will make you fishers of men.' Immediately they left their nets and followed Him." Matthew 4:19-20 (ESV)

When God calls you, it can be disruptive to your life. You'll be minding your own business and here comes Jesus calling you to Him. When He calls you, don't hesitate. Follow Him immediately. The plans you had for your life is not always what God had in mind. Do not be afraid to go wherever God leads you. Do not doubt your calling because you don't see what God sees. God will make you into the person He needs you to be. He will provide all you need. When He calls you, your job is to follow Him and He will do the rest. He will shape you into the person He called you to be. If you are afraid to go, do it anyway. Do it scared and watch how He blesses you.

Strength And Dignity

———◆———

"She is clothed with strength and dignity, and she laughs without fear of the future." Proverbs 31:25 (NLT)

God will strengthen you as you walk with Him. Every step you take forward shows strength. Every step forward means you didn't quit. God blesses those who continue walking in faith without knowing what's coming next. The longer you walk with God, the more strength you receive. Your joy grows and you are able to laugh because you have no fear of the future. You realize that the things the devil used to hurt you is actually what God is using to grow you and build your character. Learn to laugh in the midst of trouble because laughter is the best medicine for pain. Praise God in trouble because it means you are coming into a huge blessing if you don't give up.

God Is The Rock

———◆◆◆———

"Therefore everyone who hears these words of Mine and puts them into practice is like a wise man who built his house on the rock. The rain came down, the streams rose, and the winds blew and beat against that house; yet it did not fall, because it had its foundation on the rock." Matthew 7:24-25 (NIV)

It's so important to study God's Word and not to only speak it, but to put it into practice. When hard times come and struggles come, you will be able to withstand any storm that comes up against you because your foundation is the Word of God. He is the rock and if you build your house upon Him, nothing will bring it down. You will not crumble with God at the center of your life. That doesn't mean you won't fall at times, but you won't stay down.

Beautiful Creature

———◦◆◦———

"He has made everything beautiful in its time. He has also set eternity in the human heart; yet no one can fathom what God has done from the beginning to end." Ecclesiastes 3:11 (NIV)

God is a God of order. He orders your steps. His timing is always the right timing. Don't get discouraged if things aren't going the way you planned or imagined it would go. He is not finished. He is still working behind the scenes to create something beautiful. He placed eternity within your heart so you have something to strive towards. You may not quite know what your purpose is right now, but just remember that God doesn't create junk. He only creates beauty. You are coming more into your beauty everyday as He shapes you.

Grow In Faith

"The disciples went and woke Him, saying, 'Lord, save us. We're going to drown.' He replied, 'You of little faith, why are you so afraid?' Then He got up and rebuked the winds and waves, and it was completely calm." Matthew 8:25-26 (NIV)

Jesus sleeping on the boat during a storm demonstrates the kind of faith you need to have when you are going through your own storms. Remain calm and stay in peace because you know that God has given you power and authority over Satan. You have nothing to be afraid of with Christ on your side. Enjoy the freedom you have in Jesus and use the power He has given you to trample the head of Satan whenever He tries to rise up against you. We have power through the Holy Spirit. Always remember your power whenever storms rise up.

Devoted Heart

"Yet if you devote your heart to Him and stretch out your hands to Him, if you put away the sin that is in your hand and allow no evil to dwell in your tent, then, free of fault, you will lift up your face; you will stand firm and without fear." Job 11:13-15 (NIV)

God wants your whole heart, not just a piece of it. You get out whatever you put in. If you want all of Jesus, give Him all of you. Keep reaching your hands toward Him and praise Him always. Let Him cleanse you of all evil and filth so that you may be brought forth as pure gold. You can have freedom from a life of sin and misery. When things are getting difficult in your life, you will be able to stand tall and firm through it all. You don't have to fear anything or anyone. Be firm and fearless, letting nothing take your freedom.

Grieving A Loved One

———◆◆◆———

"Brothers and sisters, we do not want you to be uninformed about those who sleep in death, so that you do not grieve like the rest of mankind, who have no hope. For we believe that Jesus died and rose again, and so we believe that God will bring with Jesus, those who have fallen asleep in Him." 1 Thessalonians 4:13-14 (NIV)

As you live here on earth, you will lose people you love. It is painful, but you won't hurt like the rest of the world. You have hope because you know that you will be reunited with them again. This is not the end. They are in a better place than you are right now. Pray for the souls of those you have lost and hold on tightly to those you still have. Treasure who you still have around you in this physical world, remembering that tomorrow is not promised.

Free From Anxiety

———⊰◆⊱———

"Rejoice in the Lord always. I will say it again: Rejoice. Let your gentleness be evident to all. The Lord is near. Do not be anxious about anything, but in every situation, by prayer and petition, with thanksgiving, present your requests to God."
Philippians 4:4-6 (NIV)

Walking with the Lord makes you want to rejoice because the love you feel is indescribable. The Lord is always so close, but you have to quiet your mind and you will start to recognize Him a lot more in the things or people around you. Remain gentle in spirit and allow others to see Jesus within you. Don't worry or be anxious for anything. Ask God for whatever it is you are needing and thank Him for every situation since you know that all things work together. The Lord wants only good things for His children.

Follow The Steps Of Jesus

"To this you were called, because Christ suffered for you, leaving you an example, that you should follow in His steps. He committed no sin, and no deceit was found in His mouth. When they hurled their insults at Him, He did not retaliate; when He suffered, He made no threats. Instead, He entrusted Himself to Him who judges justly." 1 Peter 2:21-23 (NIV)

You were called by God for a time such as this. When you are suffering, although it hurts, remember Jesus suffered for you first. Follow the example of Jesus and when people persecute you by insulting you, do not get revenge on them. Give it to God and allow Him to fight your battles. Be more like Jesus and let God protect you from your enemies.

Planted By Streams

———◆———

"That person is like a tree planted by streams of water, which yields its fruit in season and whose leaf does not wither - whatever they do prospers." Psalm 1:3 (NIV)

Do not be moved by anything. Remain in the Lord and know that He has planted you right where you are supposed to be. God is bringing you into a season of harvest. Continue to sow seeds and hold on. Remaining in the Lord through good and bad weather strengthens you. Allow God to lead you into prosperity. Do not quit and you will produce good fruit in His perfect timing. This is your season, your time. God didn't say some things will prosper, He says whatever you do will prosper. Make sure you are doing good things and those good things will grow.

Good Gifts From God

————⋆◆⋆————

"If you, then, though you are evil, know how to give good gifts to your children, how much more will your Father in Heaven give good gifts to those who ask Him." Matthew 7:11 (NIV)

As parents, we love to bless our children with gifts. Seeing their beautiful faces full of joy melts our hearts. There isn't anything we wouldn't do for our children, but we try to give them things that won't hurt them. We know when to say no because everything they want may not be good for them. Our Heavenly Father is the same way with His children. He loves to bless you with gifts. He loves raining down blessings over you, but He will not give you things that will eventually hurt you. He will also teach you to work for what you want. Ask Him for the things that will help you accomplish your missions.

New Mercies Every Morning

❧

"Let the morning bring me word of Your unfailing love, for I have put my trust in You. Show me the way I should go, for to You I entrust my life." Psalm 143:8 (NIV)

Every morning introduces a new day as well as new mercies. God's love is unfailing and unconditional. He loves you so much that He allows you the chance to start fresh every morning. Yesterday is the past and if you ask God to be forgiven for any past mistakes, He will forgive you. You can't change yesterday, but ask God for His guidance today. Our Heavenly Father has created each and every one of us for a purpose. Entrust your life to Him and doors will open for you that no one will be able to shut. Run through every door God opens and whatever you do, don't look back. Praise Him and thank Him.

JUNE 29TH

Chosen And Predestined

"In Him we were also chosen, having been predestined according to the plan of Him who works out everything in conformity with the purpose of His will, in order that we, who were the first to put hope in Christ, might be for the praise of His glory." Ephesians 1:11-12 (NIV)

Before you were born, God predestined you to be apart of His plan. You were chosen by our Heavenly Father to be used as a vessel in order to bring glory to Him. He created you for something bigger. The thing that makes you stumble is the thing that God will turn around and use for His glory so that others may see the truth. God is on your side and He will work everything out for you when you choose His will for your life. Choose His way because it's beautiful and His way is always the best way.

His Way Is Higher

———◆◆◆———

"For My thoughts are not your thoughts, neither are your ways My ways,' declares the Lord. 'As the Heavens are higher than the earth, so are My ways higher than your ways and My thoughts than your thoughts." Isaiah 55:8-9 (NIV)

Things will happen on your journey through life that can be hard to comprehend. It can feel unfair whenever you fall down or lose people you love. God tells us that His thoughts and ways are higher than ours. You may not understand the reason for the things that are happening, but all things are working together for the good of those who love God. All things won't feel good at the time it's happening, but continue to hold on tightly to Him remembering that this too shall pass. God is a God of order. He has a reason for everything that happens in your life. Trust His process.

Jesus Sets Us Free

---◆◆◆---

"It is for freedom that Christ has set us free. Stand firm, then, and do not let yourselves be burdened again by a yoke of slavery." Galatians 5:1 (NIV)

We all have sin which tries to enslave us. Only you and God knows what sins you struggle with. Jesus gave the ultimate sacrifice. He gave His life and chose to die for us all so that we could be set free. Through Christ you receive your freedom from Satan and sin. Jesus broke the yoke of slavery so that you could be free to live a life of love, perfect peace, joy, confidence, and boldness in Him. Stand firm against any attack the enemy sends your way and remember that you are a child of the Most High. God gave you power over demonic spirits. You are no longer in bondage by Satan. You are free indeed.

Surviving The Wilderness

"Remember how the Lord your God led you all the way in the wilderness these forty years, to humble you and test you in order to know what was in your heart, whether or not you would keep His commands." Deuteronomy 8:2 (NIV)

We are all lost in the wilderness or in darkness at some point in our lives. No one can grow without the darker times. These times come to keep you humble so that you learn to depend on God in all you do. They come to test you in order to see what is truly in your heart. Are you a true believer in Jesus? Are you faithful to God in times of trouble? Will you continue to follow Jesus even when it gets hard or it isn't popular in the group of people you come into contact with? God will bring you into a land of prosperity if you can remain faithful to Him in a land of affliction. Hold on tightly to Him.

God Destroys Your Enemies

"The eternal God is your refuge, and underneath are the everlasting arms. He will drive out your enemies before you, saying, 'Destroy them." Deuteronomy 33:27 (NIV)

There is no reason to fear anything or anyone because God is your eternal refuge. When God has your back, there is no devil that can overtake you. He shields you from your enemies and all darkness. He is God over all things in Heaven and on earth which means nothing can rise up against you. God will destroy every spirit of darkness, deceit, or wickedness that tries to overtake your spirit. Do not be deceived by any lying spirits coming from others or within yourself. Cast down every negative thought. Remember that Jesus is your protector and your friend.

JULY 4TH

Raised For Purpose

—◆—

"For Scripture says to Pharaoh: 'I raised you up for this very purpose, that I might display My power in you and that My name might be proclaimed in all the earth." Romans 9:17 (NIV)

It doesn't feel so good to fall down, especially with people watching. It's devastating when the people you love are backing away because they don't even know how to help you. They want to help you, but sometimes it's just not possible. You have to want to change for yourself. When you fall hard enough, it will make you call out to God. He is the only One who can lift you up out of your misery and darkness. People will see His power and His glory when they see how He turned your life completely around. He will use you to show Himself mightily to others. They know it had to be God who raised you out of darkness into the light.

He Is Calling You

"Jesus stopped and said, 'Call him.' So they called to the blind man, 'Cheer up. On your feet. He's calling you." Mark 10:49 (NIV)

You are blind before God opens your eyes. You start off lost at first because you don't have any guidance. Without the guidance you need, you fall into trouble. You get into situations that are difficult because you are blind. You can't see what the truth is and you are easily deceived. God will call you to Him, but He will not force you to answer His call. He gives you free will to choose. When the pain feels bad enough, make the right choice and go to Him. Do not be afraid to come to our Heavenly Father. When He calls you, go to Him. Your life will change forever. You will finally have true peace and joy.

Sifted As Wheat

"And the Lord said, 'Simon, Simon, behold, Satan hath desired to have you, that he may sift you as wheat: But I have prayed for thee, that thy faith fail not: and when thou art converted, strengthen thy brethren." Luke 22:31-32 (KJV)

After you are walking with Jesus for awhile, you will be tested. Satan will come up against you in all kinds of ways, but you have to remain strong and hold on. No matter how difficult it may get, continue to turn to God. Satan will test you plenty. He will try to destroy your faith in God, but don't be deceived. Keep your faith and keep turning to Him because God is only allowing you to be tested to show Satan you are a true child of God. Satan cannot have you. After you have made it out of the dark, reach out to help strengthen your brothers and sisters.

What Can Mortals Do to Me?

"When I am afraid, I put my trust in You. In God, whose Word I praise - in God I trust and am not afraid. What can mere mortals do to me?" Psalm 56:3-4 (NIV)

There is no reason to fear any man or woman when God is on your side. Although people can hurt you physically or emotionally, there is still no reason to be afraid. Humans can kill the body, but they cannot kill the soul. You have to trust God and allow Him to take you wherever it is He is directing you to go. You have the Almighty, the All Powerful God on your side every step of the way. Do not be afraid of people because they do not determine your future or where your soul will go when your physical body dies. Celebrate our Heavenly Father no matter who is watching. He is number One and He will keep you.

A Faithful Servant

———◆———

"His Lord said unto him, 'Well done, good and faithful servant, thou hast been faithful over a few things; I will make thee ruler over many things: enter thou into the joy of thy Lord." Matthew 25:23 (KJV)

God will give you things to see how well you are able to handle them. He wants to see if you will be faithful over the small things before He will bless you with big things. God loves to bless His children, but He is a God of order. He will not put more on you than you can handle. He will move you up in life and make you ruler over many once you've proven yourself faithful over a few. Enter into God's joy as He blesses you.

Do Not Worry About Tomorrow

———◆———

"Therefore do not worry about tomorrow, for tomorrow will worry about itself. Each day has enough trouble of its own."
Matthew 6:34 (NIV)

We as human beings tend to worry about things we cannot fix. We have a hard time just letting things be. We don't realize that the more we try to fix what's wrong, the worse we make the situation. God makes it clear that you are to focus on the now. Let tomorrow worry about itself. Do not let the enemy steal parts of your life by distracting you with the future. Remain in your now and enjoy the present moment because usually things will not turn out as bad or at all as you imagined they would anyway. Staying focused on right now will allow you to live every moment to the fullest and will give you way more joy in the long run. Just relax.

Lord, Hear My Voice

———◆———

"Hear my cry for help, my King and my God, for to You I pray. In the morning, Lord, You hear my voice, in the morning I lay my requests before You and wait expectantly." Psalm 5:2-3 (NIV)

God hears every prayer that you send up to Him. When you pray to Him, believe that you have already received what you are praying for and wait patiently. Make it a habit to pray to Him first thing in the morning. It's very important to make time for Him as soon as you get up. Let Him guide you throughout the day. When you start with God, you start your day in love and in perfect peace. Things will still happen, but it's easier to deal with if you begin your day with God. Ask Him to guide you with His Holy Spirit. Your life will change drastically by beginning each day with Him.

Because You Love God

———◆◆◆———

"Because he loves Me," says the Lord, "I will rescue him; I will protect him, for he acknowledges My name. He will call on Me, and I will answer him; I will be with him in trouble, I will deliver him and honor him." Psalm 91:14-15 (NIV)

When you love God with all your heart, He will be with you through the good times and the bad times. If you are in any kind of trouble, God will protect you and He will deliver you. Acknowledge His name always and He will keep you. God will answer you whenever you call on Him and He will rescue you from your troubles. God will defend you from your enemies by destroying them. He will lift you up above them all. Be loyal to God even when times are more difficult. He will honor your loyalty forever.

Authority Through God

"He replied, 'I saw Satan fall like lightning from Heaven. I have given you authority to trample on snakes and scorpions and to overcome all the power of the enemy; nothing will harm you. However, do not rejoice that the spirits submit to you, but rejoice that your names are written in Heaven." Luke 10:18-20 (NIV)

God gives His children authority over darkness. Satan will use people to hurt you or to come up against you, but remain in peace knowing that darkness cannot overcome light. Part of your inheritance from our Heavenly Father is the power He gives you to trample the head of your enemies. Nothing will be able to harm you because of this power. Spirits will submit to you when you use your God-given power, but the best part is that your name is written in Heaven.

Divine Weapons

—◆—

"The weapons we fight with are not the weapons of the world. On the contrary, they have divine power to demolish strongholds. We demolish arguments and every pretension that sets itself up against the knowledge of God, and we take captive every thought to make it obedient to Christ." 2 Corinthians 10:4-5 (NIV)

You are a child of God, which means you are given a Heavenly power to overcome anything that the enemy attacks you with. It's important to read God's Word to learn the power you have in Christ. The devil attacks you in your mind a lot of the time. He will put thoughts in your head that are negative, but you have the power through Jesus to bring those thoughts into captivity, bind them up, and cast them down. Replace any negative thoughts with positive thoughts.

Radiant Light

"Those who look to Him are radiant; their faces are never covered with shame." Psalm 34:5 (NIV)

People who are walking with the Lord are full of light. The glory of the Lord shines brightly all over them. Their light radiates from within them and it cannot be hidden. Your perspective on things change when you are walking with God. You think differently. You won't worry as much because God will remind you that all things work together for the good of those who love Him and are called according to His purpose. The more you grow in Christ, the brighter the light within you shines. People around you will start to notice how radiant you are the longer you are walking with the Lord. Keep letting your light shine and don't allow anyone or anything to put it out.

God Will Uphold You

"The Lord makes firm the steps of the one who delights in Him; though he may stumble, he will not fall, for the Lord upholds him with His hand." Psalm 37:23-24 (NIV)

God has a plan for those who delight in Him and loves Him. The Lord orders your steps. He will guide you along your path toward your destiny. Along the way you will encounter troubles and may stumble, but God will hold you up to keep you from falling. Every step you climb is a victory. The Lord delights in you and He wants nothing but success for you. Allow Him to show you a better way to live. You can have real peace, real freedom, and great victory.

Perfectly United

"I appeal to you, brothers and sisters, in the name of our Lord Jesus Christ, that all of you agree with one another in what you say and that there be no divisions among you, but that you be perfectly united in mind and thought." 1 Corinthians 1:10 (NIV)

We are stronger together. It's hard to take down a whole family. If we are united as one, the enemy will have a hard time destroying one of us because he would have to destroy all of us. We have to cover one another and help strengthen each other. If we allow any division to come in between us, the enemy is able to isolate us from the rest of the family. The enemy will be successful in destroying that brother or sister. Always remember that there is strength in numbers. Remain united.

Free From The Pit

"He lifted me out of the slimy pit, out of the mud and mire;
He set my feet on a rock and gave me a firm place to stand. He
put a new song in my mouth, a hymn of praise to our God.
Many will see and fear the Lord and put their trust in Him."
Psalm 40:2-3 (NIV)

Before the Lord saves you from out of your hole, you feel like you're sinking deeper into that hole you can't climb out of. Once you finally realize that you can't save yourself, you lift your hands to the Father. Ask Him for forgiveness for all of your sins. It's ok to admit that you didn't know everything and you messed up. Now allow Him to teach you and set your feet firmly on a rock. You will find yourself singing a new song and praising Him because you are finally free. Trust Him completely.

Walk In Newness

———◆———

"Therefore we are buried with Him by baptism into death: that like as Christ was raised up from the dead by the glory of the Father, even so we also should walk in newness of life."
Romans 6:4 (KJV)

Life can be very miserable before giving your life to Christ. You are a slave to sin, which means your master is Satan. You have to die to yourself. Give your life to Christ. Allow Him to be your Master. Let God raise you up and give you a new life. Things become much more clearer and you see things in a different light. You are no longer blind. Enjoy the new eyes that God blesses you with to see how beautiful life truly is in Him.

Reap What You Sow

"Do not be deceived: God cannot be mocked. A man reaps what he sows. Whoever sows to please their flesh, from the flesh will reap destruction; whoever sows to please the Spirit, from the Spirit will reap eternal life." Galatians 6:7-8 (NIV)

You cannot pretend or hide from God. He sees everything you do. If you follow what your flesh wants, trouble will eventually come. We are all sinful by nature, which is why your flesh will lead you into destruction. It's very important to please the Spirit and not your flesh. Your flesh leads you to sin and your sin leads you to eternal death. The Spirit will lead you to eternal life. Please remember that you get whatever you put out. Let the Spirit guide you and bless you with perfect peace and joy which strengthens you.

We Are Heirs With Christ

—◦◦◦—

"The Spirit Himself testifies with our spirit that we are God's children. Now if we are children, then we are heirs - heirs of God and co-heirs with Christ, if indeed we share in His sufferings in order that we may also share in His glory."
Romans 8:16-17 (NIV)

God predestined you to be His. God made you an heir. Since you are an heir with Jesus, you will also inherit the Kingdom. When you choose God's path, you will go through trials. You will experience times of suffering. Always remember through the difficult times that Jesus suffered first so you could have freedom from the enemy. Yes, you will suffer walking with Christ, but you will also be glorified with Him. As God's child, you are a conqueror.

God Will Repay You

"God will repay each person according to what they have done. To those who by persistence in doing good seek glory, honor, and immortality, He will give eternal life. But for those who are self-seeking and who reject the truth and follow evil, there will be wrath and anger." Romans 2:6-8 (NIV)

Be careful for what you do and how you treat people. God will repay you for what you've done whether it be good or bad. Be continuous in doing good deeds. You will be glorified and honored. Being selfish, self-centered, and following evil will result in God's wrath. Make receiving eternal life your goal. Follow the truth and do the next right thing.

Shine Like The Stars

"Do everything without grumbling or arguing, so that you may become blameless and pure, children of God without fault in a warped and crooked generation. Then you will shine among them like stars in the sky as you hold firmly to the word of life. And then I will be able to boast on the day of Christ that I did not run or labor in vain." Philippians 2:14-16 (NIV)

There are times you have to do things you don't want to do. Learn to do things without complaining. Develop an attitude of gratitude by reminding yourself that there's a lot more people who are less fortunate than you. The less you argue, the more at peace you will be. The more at peace you are, the brighter your light shines. Continue to work hard for the Lord. He will greatly reward you.

Heavenly Places

"But God, who is rich in mercy, for His great love wherewith He loved us, even when we were dead in sins, hath quickened us together with Christ, (by grace ye are saved;) And hath raised us up together, and made us sit together in heavenly places in Christ Jesus." Ephesians 2:4-6 (KJV)

God raises us up from out of our graves with Jesus. By grace, God has brought you out of your sins. He has given you a new life and continues to strengthen your inner being. As you move into a new dimension of life, things that bothered you before no longer does because God's Spirit lives within you. His grace and mercy is poured out over you as you walk the path God has blessed you to walk. You are a new person and you are free to be who God created you to be. It's your choice.

JULY 24ᵀᴴ

Ever-Increasing Glory

"And we all, who with unveiled faces contemplate the Lord's glory, are being transformed into His image with ever-increasing glory, which comes from the Lord, who is the Spirit." 2 Corinthians 3:18 (NIV)

As God's child you are becoming more and more like Jesus as you follow Him. Your face glows with a beautiful radiant light because His Spirit lives within you. You are reflecting His glory. The Holy Spirit guides you from glory to glory and your light shines brighter with every step you climb up. God washes all of your sins away, cleansing you of the dirt you were once buried in. He makes you shine as pure gold after you have been made new in Christ. Shine brightly so others can see their way out of darkness by following your example.

The Lord Will Avenge

—◆◆◆—

"Do not repay anyone evil for evil. Be careful to do what is right in the eyes of everyone. If it is possible, as far as it depends on you, live at peace with everyone. Do not take revenge, my dear friends, but leave room for God's wrath, for it is written: 'It is mine to avenge; I will repay,' says the Lord."
Romans 12:17-19 (NIV)

People will hurt you in this world, even people you love and trust. Although it can be painful, God says that you are to live in peace with everyone. He will avenge you. Do not let anyone take your peace. Satan will use the people you are close with to upset you so he can take you out of your focus. That's why you have to forgive and allow God to handle the rest. Don't give the devil room to squeeze in and steal your peace. Smile and keep it moving.

Be A Lamp To Others

"You are the light of the world. A town built on a hill cannot be hidden. Neither do people light a lamp and put it under a bowl. Instead they put it on its stand, and it gives light to everyone in the house. In the same way, let your light shine before others, that they may see your good deeds and glorify your Father in Heaven." Matthew 5:14-16 (NIV)

As God's child, you have an obligation to help others see their way through the darker times. The Holy Spirit lives within you, which is why you shine brightly. God uses you as a vessel to bring love and light wherever there is hate or darkness. People will see the good you do for others and they will know that it is the Heavenly Father who moves through you. Let God use you to do great works and to lead others home to Him.

Entrust Your Life To Him

———◆———

"Let the morning bring me word of Your unfailing love, for I have put my trust in You. Show me the way I should go, for to You I entrust my life." Psalm 148:8 (NIV)

Our God is a jealous God. He wants nothing placed above Him. Not a person, a job, or anything. You may lose things that you place before Him. Put God first and He will add all the rest. Learning to spend time alone with God every morning, helps your day to go a lot smoother. Putting God's love on as a garment before you walk out your door, allows you to handle situations more wisely and with care. Ask God for direction in your life and He will answer through people, things, or in your spirit. God is your Creator so it only makes sense to ask Him what He created you for. What is your true purpose in life?

Spiritual Training

"For physical training is of some value, but godliness has value for all things, holding promise for both the present life and the life to come." 1 Timothy 4:8 (NIV)

Self-control and self-discipline is definitely worth practicing. There are certain things that are good to avoid because those things could lead you back into a life full of sin. The physical things are important, but your spiritual well-being has more importance and value than anything. The more you train yourself spiritually, the stronger you will be. Allow yourself to grow stronger through God's Word. His Word is powerful and it takes precedence over all things. Make your physical training a goal, but make your spiritual training your mission.

You Know Me Lord

—◆◇◆—

"You have searched me, Lord, and You know me. You know when I sit and when I rise; You perceive my thoughts from afar. You discern my going out and my lying down; You are familiar with all my ways." Psalm 139:1-3 (NIV)

There is nothing that the Lord doesn't know about you. He wrote your story. He knows everything you think and He knows everything you're about to do before it even happens. He is light and He illuminates every dark place in your life. Instead of trying to hide your sins from Him, go to Him and confess them. Ask Him for forgiveness and allow Him to bless you with a fresh start. You can't change what you won't admit. Everyone stumbles sometimes, but allow God to pick you up and dust you off. After He pulls you back up, keep walking in your purpose toward your destination.

Refined In The Fire

"But He knoweth the way that I take: when He hath tried me, I shall come forth as gold." Job 23:10 (KJV)

Following Jesus is not always easy. Although things can get tough at times, don't give up. God created your path. Turn to Him for guidance and He will show you the right way to go. As you follow Jesus, trials will come to test you. The closer you get to your destination, the harder the trials become. Celebrate in the tough times knowing that you are closer than you've ever been. No one can come forth as pure gold without being refined by fire. You are beginning to shine brighter everyday as you conquer each battle you face. You are a true warrior.

I Will Not Be Shaken

"I keep my eyes always on the Lord. With Him at my right hand, I will not be shaken. Therefore my heart is glad and my tongue rejoices; my body also will rest secure, because You will not abandon me to the realm of the dead, nor will You let Your faithful one see decay." Psalm 16:8-10 (NIV)

When trials come to test you it can be difficult, but don't take your eyes off of the Lord. If you focus on Him, nothing can shake you. God will bless you with power, protection, and provision. He will not abandon you if you're loyal and faithful to Him. Whatever kills your flesh is your sacrifice. Remain in God even when it hurts and He will honor your sacrifice. God will exalt you in His Kingdom if you remain loyal. Stay true to God and let nothing shake you away from Him.

AUGUST 1ˢᵀ

Healed By His Wounds

———⋄———

"Surely He took up our pain and bore our suffering, yet we considered Him punished by God, stricken by Him, and afflicted. But He was pierced for our transgressions, He was crushed for our iniquities; the punishment that brought us peace was on Him, and by His wounds we are healed." Isaiah 53:4-5 (NIV)

There is no need to continue punishing yourself for past mistakes. Once you come to Jesus, you are washed in His blood. You are made new. Jesus took all of your sins on Him so you could be made righteous. He has conquered death so you can now experience peace through the Holy Spirit. Don't allow the devil to deceive you. You're healed by the stripes Jesus took for you. He took all of your pain and suffering on Him so don't take it back. Live in your freedom through Christ.

God Will Not Forsake You

"No one will be able to stand against you all the days of your life. As I was with Moses, so I will be with you; I will never leave you nor forsake you." Joshua 1:5 (NIV)

As a child of God, you are completely protected under the blood of Jesus. God will not let anyone come up against you. Nothing will overcome you if you remain in Him. God fights for His children. You don't have to get revenge on anyone because in God's perfect timing, He will avenge you. God is a great Father and He will never leave you. His hand is always holding you up and guiding you through the wilderness. God is silent at times, but it's not because He isn't there. Our faith is tested in how we handle the silence. Remember that God is with you always, even when He is silent. Remain faithful.

Apple of God's Eye

"Keep me as the apple of Your eye; hide me in the shadow of Your wings from the wicked who are out to destroy me, from my mortal enemies who surround me." Psalm 17:8-9 (NIV)

You are the apple of our Heavenly Father's eye. Like a mother eagle covers her eaglet when it's first born, God covers you with His wings. He protects you from any kind of wickedness or from any enemies that come up against you. He keeps you in His nest for a while as He grows you and feed you until you are strong. The mother eagle will drop her eaglet off a cliff, but not to kill it. She does this to make the eaglet learn how to flap its wings and fly. God will also drop you in your scary place in order for you to find your wings and learn to fly. Don't be afraid of anything. Spread your wings and soar.

God Is Gracious

———◆———

"Even now," declares the Lord, "return to Me with all your heart, with fasting and weeping and mourning." Rend your heart and not your garments. Return to the Lord your God, for He is gracious and compassionate, slow to anger and abounding in love, and He relents from sending calamity." Joel 2:12-13 (NIV)

As you walk the path God has blessed you to walk, you may backslide at times.. Do not give up if you backslide because God is a very loving God and He will forgive you. He will not send a great disaster against you because He knows your heart. He blesses you with grace and wants you to return to Him even after you stumble. If you fall, get back up and fight for your life.

AUGUST 5TH

Strong And Courageous

———◆———

"Have I not commanded you? Be strong and courageous. Do not be afraid; do not be discouraged, for the Lord your God will be with you wherever you go." Joshua 1:9 (NIV)

Being apart of God's family is such a blessing. He is always with you wherever you are. He commands you to be strong and have courage. You have the Almighty God dwelling within you. You cannot let fear overcome you. Do not be afraid of anything because God is all powerful and His Spirit works through you everyday. Look fear in the face and destroy it by letting the light within you shine brighter than the darkness fear brings. You have the same power flowing within you that Jesus used to conquer death. Use the power God gave you to do great and wonderful things.

Be Still And Wait

———◦◦◦———

"Be still before the Lord and wait patiently for Him; do not fret when people succeed in their ways, when they carry out their wicked schemes." Psalm 37:7 (NIV)

The people of God prospers in His perfect timing. Wait on Him to move you into blessings. There is a process we all must go through before we experience our highest success. Anything you get too fast can overwhelm you and may set you back. Trust His process completely. You may not get what you want right away, but that doesn't mean you won't get it later down the line. God loves to see His children happy and He will give you the desires of your heart according to His will. Don't faint in the process and watch God bless you beyond your wildest dreams.

AUGUST 7ᵀᴴ

Passing Judgement

———◆———

"Therefore let us stop passing judgement on one another. Instead, make up your mind not to put any stumbling block or obstacle in the way of a brother or sister." Romans 14:13 (NIV)

There is only one perfect human being that ever lived and His name is Jesus. Along your path towards your destination, things will come to trip you up. Sometimes those things succeed and other times you climb right over it. If you fall, get up and keep it moving. When you get up, remember how it felt to fall the next time your brother or sister falls. Don't be so quick to judge the next person since we all fall at times. Instead of putting an obstacle in their path, reach out your hand to help them back up. We are all family running toward the finish line. Let's get there together.

Power Of The Tongue

"From the fruit of their mouth a person's stomach is filled; with the harvest of their lips they are satisfied. The tongue has the power of life and death, and those who love it will eat its fruit." Proverbs 18:20-21 (NIV)

Words are very powerful. You come from a Father who speaks things into existence and since you are His child, you have the same power. It's very important to watch what you say to yourself and to other people. You have the power to speak life to your brothers' and sisters' spirits. When you speak, let your words edify others. Your words can also tear someone down and set them back. Practice speaking only good things over yourself and others. Remember that successful people build other successful people up. Speak life over at least one person you love today.

Overflowing With Hope

"May the God of hope fill you with all joy and peace as you trust in Him, so that you may overflow with hope by the power of the Holy Spirit." Romans 15:13 (NIV)

We all have dreams. It doesn't matter how young or old you are. You can dream no matter what age you are. God will overflow you with peace and joy as you trust Him, believing He can do anything you ask Him to do. God will overflow you with hope, blessing you with the power of the Holy Spirit which will guide you along your path toward your dreams. Believe in yourself and don't stop chasing after your dreams. God will make every dream you have come true, but you have to have faith. You have to also meet Him halfway by taking action. Know that God can and will do the impossible, but you have to believe it.

Heritage Of Servants

—◆—

"No weapon formed against you shall prosper, and every tongue which rises against you in judgement you shall condemn. This is the heritage of the servants of the Lord, and their righteousness is from Me," says the Lord. Isaiah 54:17 (NKJV)

Not one thing your enemy sends against you will prosper. Not one word spoken against you will succeed. As God's child, you inherit His righteousness. God will not let your enemies have victory over you. He will fight every battle that rises against you. Be still and let God avenge you. He has a protective shield over you. Refrain from getting upset and losing your peace because God will not allow you to suffer any attack from your enemies. You can relax because as God's child, you are given the victory over all your enemies.

God Is Keeping You

"When you pass through the waters, I will be with you; and when you pass through the rivers, they will not sweep over you. When you walk through the fire, you will not be burned; the flames will not set you ablaze." Isaiah 43:2 (NIV)

It's a wonderful feeling to know that God is with you wherever you are. Your mind is put at ease when you begin to understand that God will not let you drown or be burned by fire. You may not feel great all the time when you're going through tough situations, but don't get discouraged. As God's child, you know, that you know, that you know, He will never let anything take you down. You may stumble a bit, but you will not be destroyed because of who your Father is. Stay encouraged in all you do. Many blessings to you.

God's Discipline

———◆———

*"They disciplined us for a little while as they thought best;
but God disciplines us for our good, in order that we may
share in His holiness. No discipline seems pleasant at the
time, but painful. Later on, however, it produces a harvest of
righteousness and peace for those who have been trained by it."
Hebrews 12:10-11 (NIV)*

You are blessed to have the people in your life
who help discipline you. Now God is training you
through trials to grow you into His goodness and His
holiness. The trials are used to rid you of the things
which separate you from God. He rewards you with
righteousness and peace as you grow. You are blessed
to be chosen by God who is now creating you into a
beautiful masterpiece. Trust the process and allow God
to reveal to you who you were meant to be.

AUGUST 13ᵀᴴ

The Light Of Life

"When Jesus spoke again to the people, He said, 'I am the light of the world. Whoever follows Me will never walk in darkness, but will have the light of life." John 8:12 (NIV)

Darkness cannot overcome light. Wherever there is light, darkness cannot remain. Jesus is the light of the world. You cannot see your way out of darkness without Him being a lamp to your feet. You are given the choice whether you want to stay blind or to receive your sight. Make the best choice. Follow Jesus who is the light of life and you will never walk in darkness. Let the Truth guide you as you navigate your way through a world full of darkness and deceit. Jesus is your navigator and He is directing you back to your Home. Enjoy His warm love and light as He leads the way.

Stand Firm In Christ

—◆—

"Therefore, my dear brothers and sisters, stand firm. Let nothing move you. Always give yourselves fully to the work of the Lord, because you know that your labor in the Lord is not in vain." 1 Corinthians 15:58 (NIV)

When you are God's child, you have the right to win. That doesn't mean things won't come to shake your faith, but you have to stand firm without being moved. Don't believe any depressing or suicidal spirits that come to upset you. Tell them to go. You have power in your tongue and what you speak will form. As you do the Lord's work, give your all. Throw your whole self at it. Whatever you throw yourself at, throws itself back to you. Be watchful of the things that come to test your faith. Don't be moved by anything. In the storm, stand firmly in Christ.

Pray In Secret

———◆———

"But when you pray, go into your room, close the door and pray to your Father, who is unseen. Then your Father, who sees what is done in secret, will reward you." Matthew 6:6 (NIV)

The connection you have with God is the most important connection you will ever have. He is the One who has the power to prosper you in all areas of your life. It's vital that you grow in your relationship with God. Like any relationship, communication is key. You can only build a great relationship through communication and trust. Set aside some time just for God. Pray to Him and ask Him for guidance. Ask and believe you have already received what you've asked for. He will reward you for what you've done in secret by answering your prayers according to His will.

Comfort Others

"Praise be to the God and Father of our Lord Jesus Christ, the Father of compassion and the God of all comfort, who comforts us in all our troubles, so that we can comfort those in any trouble with the comfort we ourselves receive from God."
2 Corinthians 1:3-4 (NIV)

Life is not always going to be easy. Trouble will come sometimes, but you have the Father there to comfort you through it all. He shows compassion and He gives you grace. You are becoming more and more like Him everyday the closer you get to Him. Since you are His children, you should give the same comfort and compassion to others that you receive from our Father. Be a strong support for your brothers and sisters when they are suffering. Help them get back up and stand strong together.

AUGUST 17ᵀᴴ

Good Thoughts

"Finally, brothers and sisters, whatever is true, whatever is noble, whatever is right, whatever is pure, whatever is lovely, whatever is admirable - if anything is excellent or praiseworthy - think about such things." Philippians 4:8 (NIV)

The way you think affects the way your life will go. What you think about will eventually manifest. Cast down negative thoughts and replace them with positive thoughts. Think on good, honest, pure, and lovely things. God's Word is light. Learn His Word. Do what it says and your life will begin to feel like a great dream. You will notice fear and darkness fading away as you are being overflowed with God's love and light. Your wings will slowly manifest as you prepare for liftoff. Fly into the next dimension of life.

Be Fearless

"But now, this is what the Lord says - He who created you, Jacob, He who formed you, Israel: 'Do not fear, for I have redeemed you; I have summoned you by name; you are Mine." Isaiah 43:1 (NIV)

You can live your life fearless because of who your Father is. God has saved you from the evils of this world. He has raised you up for this very moment for a special purpose. When God is ready for you, there is no place you can hide from Him. Stop running from the One who created you. Let Him finish the work He has started in you. He will call you by name to Himself. Nothing will be able to stop Him from getting to you because you are His. God is taking you through a process to mold you into the most beautiful masterpiece He created you to be. Remain fearless.

AUGUST 19TH

Counted As Worthy

———⚬———

"Therefore, among God's churches we boast about your perseverance and faith in all the persecutions and trials you are enduring. All this is evidence that God's judgement is right, and as a result you will be counted worthy of the Kingdom of God, for which you are suffering." 2 Thessalonians 1:4-5 (NIV)

As trials and persecutions come, hold on to your faith. Remember that all things are working together. Pain produces power. You are maturing, growing stronger, and wiser through every battle you fight. Trials produce good character as you learn what works and what doesn't. Be willing to change the things that aren't helping you succeed in life. God knows exactly what you need to be counted worthy in His Kingdom. Trust His process. He will not let you fall.

AUGUST 20TH

Waiting On God

"Be still before the Lord and wait patiently for Him; do not fret when people succeed in their ways, when they carry out their wicked schemes." Psalm 37:7 (NIV)

Waiting patiently for the Lord to move is not always easy, but it's necessary. Things you get too fast can overwhelm you. Your character may not be developed enough to hold on to the thing you want the most. Anything you receive by fighting, you will also fight to keep. You will value anything you have to fight for a lot more than if it was handed to you. The wicked may get things faster than you, but that's not your business. Let God be God and allow Him to deal with those people. You need to focus on what God wants you to do to prosper. Stay focused on the goal set before you and arrive in God's perfect timing.

AUGUST 21ST

Access Granted

———◄◆►———

"At that moment the curtain of the temple was torn in two from top to bottom. The earth shook, the rocks split and the tombs broke open. The bodies of many holy people who had died were raised to life." Matthew 27:51-52 (NIV)

When Jesus sacrificed His life on the cross, the veil was torn from top to bottom. It was torn giving us access to God. You can now come boldly to His throne and have a relationship with Him. There is nothing standing in between us and God because of what Jesus did on the cross. Jesus has already done the work for us defeating Satan. The devil has no power over you. Don't let him deceive you. You are God's child and He has granted you access. ACCESS GRANTED.

Stop Your Worrying

———◆◆◆———

"Therefore I tell you, do not worry about your life, what you will eat or drink; or about your body, what you will wear. Is not life more than food, and the body more than clothes? Look at the birds of the air; they do not sow or reap or store away in barns; and yet your Heavenly Father feeds them. Are you not much more valuable than they? Can any one of you by worrying add a single hour to your life?" Matthew 6:25-34 (NIV)

The devil can't take the blessings God has for you so he tries to distract your mind with worry. Your mind is the most powerful weapon you have. If Satan can worry your mind with the future, he takes your power. Satan takes you out of your peace if he can worry you. If the devil can make you live in the past or the future, he takes parts of your life and also your joy. God makes it clear that He comes to give us life more abundantly. Do not worry about anything. Nothing will change if you sit and worry about your future so live in the moment and work on whatever you are able to work on today. If you work on today, you won't have too much trouble in the future.

AUGUST 23RD

Eternal Spiritual Benefits

———◆———

"Jesus answered, 'Very truly I tell you, you are looking for Me, not because you saw the signs I performed but because you ate the loaves and had your fill. Do not work for food that spoils, but for food that endures to eternal life, which the Son of Man will give you. For on Him God the Father has placed His seal of approval." John 6:26-27 (NIV)

When you follow Jesus, miracles will happen in your life. Be careful not to follow Jesus because of the physical benefits. These are temporary things which have no use in the afterlife. Follow Jesus because of the eternal life you will receive. His way is the best way and the right way. Don't allow the physical things to distract you from your spiritual needs. Be filled spiritually by following Jesus and everything else will be added to you as you walk toward your purpose.

Sit With Jesus

"To the one who is victorious, I will give the right to sit with Me on My throne, just as I was victorious and sat down with My Father on His throne." Revelation 3:21 (NIV)

Winning requires a lot of hard work. It takes practice to become victorious in anything you do. As you face certain difficulties, you may stumble a bit. If you fail at something, get back up and try again. It's important to learn from every failure. Make the changes necessary to become victorious. As you go through life, you will begin learning from your mistakes a lot quicker. Keep in mind that your prize for being victorious in your life is huge. Jesus says that the one who is victorious will sit with Him on His throne. That is the best prize you could ever win.

AUGUST 25TH

Winning Souls

"Though I am free and belong to no one, I have made myself a slave to everyone, to win as many as possible." 1 Corinthians 9:19 (NIV)

You are made free through Christ. He died to free you from sin. Although you are free, you must still serve all people. You have to be interested and feed what's in someone else in order to gain their attention. Once you have their attention, you have a chance to win them over. They will open their heart toward you and listen to the truth when you speak it. Let them see what Christ has done for you in your life so that they may also glorify our Father in Heaven. None of us know the day or the hour Christ is coming back. Make it your mission to win as many souls as you possibly can.

Conviction Not Condemnation

———⟨⟩———

"When they kept on questioning Him, He straightened up and said to them, 'Let any one of you who is without sin be the first to throw a stone at her." John 8:7 (NIV)

When others make mistakes or they fall, do you condemn them? Jesus doesn't condemn you when you do wrong. You are convicted, not condemned. Conviction means you're declared guilty, but condemnation is a very strong disapproval. If you're convicted, you are given the opportunity to change what you've done wrong. If you are condemned, you are punished. Jesus wants you to become a better person. He did not come to punish you. Since He doesn't condemn us, you shouldn't condemn others either. It is not your place to punish others, but to help them back up so they too can become great people in God's Kingdom.

He Frees Our Feet

"The Lord confides in those who fear Him; He makes His covenant known to them. My eyes are ever on the Lord, for only He will release my feet from the snare." Psalm 25:14-15 (NIV)

As you follow Jesus, you become His friend and apart of His Royal Family. He tells you His secrets as you come into agreement and alignment with His will for your life. The enemy will send attack against you in order to distract you from your life mission or to trap you, but it's your job to keep your eyes on the Lord. Stay focused on Jesus and pray to Him when distractions come because He is the only One who is able to free you from these traps. Trust His way and His guidance.

Press On Toward The Prize

"Brothers and sisters, I do not consider myself yet to have taken hold of it. But one thing I do: Forgetting what is behind and straining toward what is ahead, I press on toward the goal to win the prize for which God has called me Heavenward in Christ Jesus." Philippians 3:13-14 (NIV)

Remain humble and open to God's direction as you move ahead. Don't let your past mistakes rule your thoughts. Learn from your past and keep pressing forward as you reach toward the main goal. Finish the race and win the prize God has called you to in Heaven. It's not important if you finish the race fast, but it's crucial to continue pressing toward the mark and to finish the race strong.

AUGUST 29TH

The Light From His Face

"Many, Lord, are asking, 'Who will bring us prosperity?' Let the light of Your face shine on us. Fill my heart with joy when their grain and new wine abound. In peace I will lie down and sleep, for You alone, Lord, make me dwell in safety." Psalm 4:6-8 (NIV)

God's light shines brightly on you and His goodness will manifest in your life every single day as you continue in His way. The joy He overflows you with begins to spill over into the lives of those who are placed in your path. You are blessed with a peace, which surpasses all understanding. This kind of peace you receive from the Lord cannot be taken by anyone or any circumstance. When you close your eyes at night, you will feel completely safe. You know our Father in Heaven has you covered and hidden underneath His wings.

Be Strong, Don't Give Up

―――◦◆◦―――

"But as for you, be strong and do not give up, for your work will be rewarded." 2 Chronicles 15:7 (NIV)

At times you may feel that all you are doing in the Kingdom is for nothing. Situations may get really tough to handle and you may feel like quitting. Don't give in to the feeling. Keep striving to do what you know is right. Remember that the difficulties are only used to produce strength and character. Power is produced from pain. Remain strong in these moments and if you don't give up, God will reward your work. All things are working together to produce the best version of yourself. Don't get discouraged when trouble comes, but rejoice because you know that God is growing you to greatness.

The Lord Lifts Up a Standard

"So shall they fear the name of the Lord from the west, and His glory from the rising of the sun. When the enemy shall come in like a flood, the Spirit of the Lord shall lift up a standard against him." Isaiah 59:19 (KJV)

There are times when you feel very overwhelmed. It feels like everything that can go wrong, does go wrong. The enemy sends a great attack against you and you feel like you can't get out of his grip. While going through these times, call out the name of Jesus. Believe that God will keep you. He will not let you be tempted beyond measure. God will protect you from the enemy and his attacks. Wherever there is light, darkness must go. Fill yourself up with the light of God's Word. Be comforted knowing that if God is for you, no one can be against you.

SEPTEMBER 1ST

Tomorrow Is Not Promised

———❖———

"Now listen, you who say, 'Today or tomorrow we will go to this or that city, spend a year there, carry on business and make money.' Why, you do not even know what will happen tomorrow. What is your life? You are a mist that appears for a little while and then vanishes. Instead, you ought to say, 'If it is the Lord's will, we will live and do this or that." James 4:13-15 (NIV)

Tomorrow is a mystery. You will wake up in the morning and have no idea what the day will bring. You make plans, but you don't really know if those plans will hold up or change. Remain flexible and open to the adventure life brings you. Hold on to Jesus and enjoy the ride. Allow the Holy Spirit to lead you. Life is short so live it to the fullest. Leave a great legacy for the ones who are coming after you.

Chosen Out Of The World

"If the world hates you, keep in mind that it hated Me first. If you belonged to the world, it would love you as its own. As it is, you do not belong to the world, but I have chosen you out of the world. That is why the world hates you." John 15:18-19 (NIV)

You will come across haters in this world, people who hate you without cause. Jesus says it's because you have been chosen by Him. He reminds us that He was hated first. When your enemies come up against you, bless them as the Word tells you to do. God has chosen you out of the world to be His own. Remember that you won't always fit in with the crowd because you are unique. You were created to do special things here on earth. The next time someone hates on you, smile because you know it means you were chosen.

Being Used To Save Many Lives

"*You intended to harm me, but God intended it for good to accomplish what is now being done, the saving of many lives.*"
Genesis 50:20 (NIV)

Satan comes to destroy you. He will use people you love to hurt you. He will bring calamity upon you any way possible. After you have been broken by the devil, God will slowly put you back together again piece by piece, if you allow Him to do so. He gives you the choice to continue to be dragged through the mud or to surrender to Him. If you choose to surrender, He will use you to help save many lives from the thing that broke you. God allowed Satan to break you so that He could use you for the glory of His Kingdom. You are blessed.

SEPTEMBER 4TH

Remain At The Lord's Feet

———◆———

"She had a sister called Mary, who sat at the Lord's feet listening to what He said. But Martha was distracted by all the preparations that had to be made. She came to Him and asked, 'Lord, don't You care that my sister has left me to do the work by myself? Tell her to help me.' 'Martha, Martha,' the Lord answered, 'you are worried and upset about many things, but few things are needed - or indeed only one. Mary has chosen what is better, and it will not be taken away from her." Luke 10:39-42 (NIV)

Be careful not to let the distractions of the world keep you from having a close relationship with God. It's important to be still. Listen to God's teaching and guidance before you go out into the world. God will not steer you wrong. If you sit still and quiet your mind at some point in the day everyday, you will hear God speak to you. He will light the way for your feet as He guides you to places He wants you to go to do great works and He will reward you for the great work you do. The best choice you can make is to remain at the Lord's feet.

SEPTEMBER 5ᵀᴴ

Be Wise And Listen To Advice

———◆———

"The way of fools seems right to them, but the wise listen to advice." Proverbs 12:15 (NIV)

God will place people in your path that He will speak through to you. Be willing to listen to the advice of God's children. Don't do things the way you have always done them. Don't be fooled by doing what only seems right to you. You can't always go with how you feel. It's not in the feeling, it's in the knowing. Push past the way you feel. Do what you know you need to do in order for your life to change. God knows everything. Be open to the advice of people God has placed in your life. It's exciting when you see your life changing for the better. You are a new person with a brand new life.

Rooted And Built Up In Him

"So then, just as you received Christ Jesus as Lord, continue to live your lives in Him, rooted and built up in Him, strengthened in the faith as you were taught, and overflowing with thankfulness." Colossians 2:6-7 (NIV)

After you receive Christ as your Lord and Savior, you become apart of His Royal Family. You're anchored in Jesus and you are strengthened as you grow in Christ. Your faith becomes stronger as you begin to see Him working in your life from glory to glory. Instead of being worried or fearful about the next steps in your life, you become more relaxed because you understand that if God did that, then He will also do this. Your gratitude overflows bringing more and more goodness into your life. Remain grateful because God's children want for nothing.

Leave Room For God's Wrath

"Do not take revenge, My dear friends, but leave room for God's wrath, for it is written: 'It is Mine to avenge; I will repay,' says the Lord. On the contrary: 'If your enemy is hungry, feed him; if he is thirsty, give him something to drink. In doing this, you will heap burning coals on his head.' Do not be overcome by evil, but overcome evil with good." Romans 20:19-21 (NIV)

Being a Christian doesn't mean you won't have anger, but don't let it have you. As you grow in your walk with God, He will teach you how to fight. People will upset you at times, but don't fight them. Fight the devil behind them that is using them to come against you. Remember that it is not your battle, it is the Lord's battle. Pray for the person, bless them. The Lord will win you the victory.

SEPTEMBER 8ᵀᴴ

Focus On Your Own Journey

"When Peter saw Him, he asked, 'Lord, what about him?' Jesus answered, 'If I want him to remain alive until I return, what is that to you? You must follow Me?" John 21:21-22 (NIV)

In this verse, Peter asked Jesus how John would die. Instead of Jesus telling Peter, He let Peter know that it wasn't his business. You are to teach the Word to feed others, but their journey is not your business. Allow God to do the changing of their heart. You need to be focused on your own walk with God. Everyone learns in their own way in their own time. Don't make anyone feel guilty about their walk with God. Your job is to focus on Jesus and to follow Him. Pray for His children and make yourself available if they come to you for help. God will do the changing.

God's Children Overcomes

———◆———

"In fact, this is love for God: to keep His commands. And His commands are not burdensome, for everyone born of God overcomes the world. This is the victory that has overcome the world, even our faith." 1 John 5:3-4 (NIV)

Life becomes easier to live once you follow God's direction. When you truly love God, you want to follow His commands as your love for Him grows daily. There is no need to be fearful because you are born of God and you are victorious. You will overcome anything the enemy tries to plant in your life. Keep your faith in every situation and God will bring you through it all. You are more than a conqueror in Christ, you are a champion. You will win.

Don't Lose Your Head

"Take the helmet of salvation and the sword of the Spirit, which is the Word of God." Ephesians 6:17 (NIV)

Difficult situations will come at different stages of your life, but you can't lose your head. When stressful situations rise up, remain calm. Speak God's Word out loud so the enemy can't deceive you or confuse you. You can't think rationally when you're worried, which is why the enemy puts worrisome thoughts in your head. Keep a clear mind by casting down every negative thought that enters your mind. God says, "NO WEAPON FORMED AGAINST YOU SHALL PROSPER." You can't always use your heart to make decisions, you must use your head to make rational decisions to climb the mountain ahead of you. A clear sober mind helps you to make great life decisions allowing you to reach the top.

SEPTEMBER 11ᵀᴴ

God Promised He Would

———◆———

"I am with you and will watch over you wherever you go, and I will bring you back to this land. I will not leave you until I have done what I have promised you." Genesis 28:15 (NIV)

God promises that He will be with you wherever your feet walk. He is watching over you, protecting you. There is no reason to fear the next step in your life because you have the "BIG BOSS" guiding you wherever you go. God said that He will not leave you until He does what He promised you. You don't have to conform to the world in order to fit in with them. You don't have to kiss up to anyone in order to be successful. Whatever God gives you, cannot be taken from you. Be yourself and do you. No one can beat you at doing you. God created you for a special purpose and it can only be done by you.

We Are God's Handiwork

"For we are God's handiwork, created in Christ Jesus to do good works, which God prepared in advance for us to do."
Ephesians 2:10 (NIV)

God created each one of us for a specific purpose to do a specific thing for the glory of His Kingdom. It is important to be who He created you to be instead of trying to be what someone else believes you should be. God did not create you to do the works of others. He created you to do great works for His Kingdom. The only way to become great at what you do is to overcome the limitations placed on you by others. When you're true to yourself, you have fewer limitations because you're not doing things the way the world says you should do them. Get excited about your uniqueness and who you are. You're a diamond, shine brightly.

God fulfills His Promises

———◄◆►———

"God is not human, that He should lie, not a human being, that He should change His mind. Does He speak and then not act? Does He promise and not fulfill?" Numbers 23:19 (NIV)

God cannot lie. If He speaks something, it will come to pass. He created each one of us to do something special for His Kingdom. Once He promises something, He will not change His mind. You may be delayed on your journey, but you will be who God said you will be. It is a process to create a perfected work. Continue to tell God that you trust Him even when it looks bad. You know that He will do what He said He will do. Continue walking with Him by faith because you have a divine appointment with destiny. You will become who God said you are in Christ. Keep walking in His promises.

SEPTEMBER 14ᵀᴴ

Strong, Firm, and Steadfast

———⊷◆⊶———

"And the God of all grace, who called you to His eternal glory in Christ, after you have suffered a little while, will Himself restore you and make you strong, firm, and steadfast." 1 Peter 5:10 (NIV)

God calls you to His eternal glory. Once He calls you, He will allow you to suffer and experience pain, but it's not to hurt you. He does this in order to strengthen you for what He's called you to. If you can stand up against the tests, He will restore you. Your life will change. You will be stronger, dependable, and firm. Storms will not break you so easily. Allow the pain to make you stronger, not a monster. If you fall, get up and try again. There is no failure, but only life lessons. Be willing to learn from what tripped you up. Be grateful for God's grace.

God Hates Your Sin, Not You

———◆———

"There are six things the Lord hates, seven that are detestable to Him: haughty eyes, a lying tongue, hands that shed innocent blood, a heart that devises wicked schemes, feet that are quick to rush into evil, a false witness who pours out lies and a person who stirs up conflict in the community." Proverbs 6:16-19 (NIV)

There's no one person who is perfect, except Jesus Christ. We've all sinned in some way, but God doesn't hate you because of your sins. He gave His only Son to clear you of the charges against you. God hates what you've done, but He doesn't hate you. He loves you. If God isn't condemning you, why are you still condemning you? Begin again and watch how God blesses you. You are fearfully and wonderfully made. Now it's time to walk in that truth.

Don't Question God

"But who are you, a human being, to talk back to God? Shall what is formed say to the One who formed it, 'Why did You make me like this?' Does not the Potter have the right to make out of the same lump of clay some pottery for special purposes and some for common use?" Romans 9:20-21 (NIV)

We as human beings can't understand the ways of God because His ways and thoughts are higher than ours. Although you may not understand why certain things are happening, walk in faith toward the next thing God has prepared for you. Everyone of us are used for His purpose even when we don't feel like we have much value. Don't question the One who created you. He knows exactly what you need to get you through each dimension in your life to accomplish your life mission.

SEPTEMBER 17TH

Overlook the Offense

"The discretion of a man deferreth his anger; and it is his glory to pass over a transgression." Proverbs 19:11 (KJV)

People will hurt you at some point in your life, but those experiences come to strengthen you. Be slow to anger and remember that God will avenge you. Keep yourself from falling into any trap that the enemy sets for your feet to take your peace. If you are wise, you will be patient and allow God to be God. Let God fight your battles. You are stronger when you can forgive others for the evil they have done to you. You don't have to continue to let them hurt you, but it's important to let go and let God take matters into His own hands. Keep your peace with everyone no matter what and God will bless your situation.

SEPTEMBER 18ᵀᴴ

Allegiance to God

"But thanks be to God that, though you used to be slaves to sin, you have come to obey from your heart the pattern of teaching that has now claimed your allegiance." Romans 6:17 (NIV)

Remain grateful to be free from the grip of your old master, sin. Before coming to God, you were dead in your sins, which turned you into a slave. No one who lived in darkness, wanted anything to do with the light because they didn't want to expose their truth since it was so painful. Now that you have chosen to die with Christ, you are raised with Him and are free to live in the light. You are no longer afraid of life. Continue living in His freedom and enjoy being a servant of righteousness. Life feels more like a great adventure now instead of a painful experience. Enjoy the ride with Christ.

Spirit of Freedom

—◆—

"Now the Lord is the Spirit, and where the Spirit of the Lord is, there is freedom. And we all, who with unveiled faces contemplate the Lord's glory, are being transformed into His image with ever-increasing glory, which comes from the Lord, who is the Spirit." 2 Corinthians 3:17-18 (NIV)

Your life will change completely when you allow God to free you from sin. People will begin to notice your transformation as they see the glory of the Lord all over you. They can see God's light through you. God pours out His Spirit on you when you are open to change and open to better. He will not force anything on you. He gives you the choice to walk in the Spirit of His freedom. Darkness will begin to fade as you open your heart to the light of His Word. Choose to be free.

Giving in the Spirit

———◆———

"There will always be poor people in the land. Therefore I command you to be open handed toward your fellow Israelites who are poor and needy in your land." Deuteronomy 15:11 (NIV)

God did not design you to do life alone. He wants His people to come together and help one another. When you see someone struggling to get ahead, help them up. You may not have a lot yourself, but if you trust God and help someone else less fortunate than you, He will sustain you. God will give you what you give Him. Trust God enough to allow Him to guide you in giving to His children. He will not allow you to go without. We are a lot stronger together. You get whatever you give so make sure you are giving abundantly and you will also receive abundantly.

SEPTEMBER 21ST

The Spirit of Teamwork

———◆———

"Moses' father-in-law replied, 'What you are doing is not good. You and these people who come to you will only wear yourselves out. The work is too heavy for you; you cannot handle it alone." Exodus 18:17-18 (NIV)

God gives us missions to accomplish on earth. It's exciting to be given great tasks from Him, but certain missions can be too much for you to accomplish alone. It can wear you down if you're not careful. That's why relationships with others are important. You get so much more done when you are able to work as a team. You may not like everything someone does, but keep the peace between you all because God's plan is much greater than any offense you could ever have against your brother or sister. Find ways to work with all people to complete God's work.

SEPTEMBER 22ND

Lack of Counsel

"Without counsel purposes are disappointed: but in the multitude of counsellors they are established." Proverbs 15:22 (KJV)

It's important to follow your dreams. On your journey toward your dreams, you will have some twists and turns. That's why it's crucial to have great people you truly trust who can give you good advice as you continue on your path. Passion without process can be a bad thing. Process allows you to stand firm and allows you to learn important lessons while going after your dreams. Process also allows you to become a master at what you have passion for. Be patient and be open to the wisdom of those who have gone before you. Learn from the mistakes of others instead of wasting valuable time having to learn the same lessons yourself. God puts many counselors in your path, listen closely while using discernment.

Lord, In The Morning

"My voice shalt thou hear in the morning, O Lord, in the morning will I direct my prayer unto thee, and will look up."
Psalm 5:3 (KJV)

Make it a habit to spend time with our Creator, the Most High, every morning when you open your eyes. Come to Him, thanking Him for another day and ask Him for whatever you are needing. After you ask Him for what it is you need, be patient and wait for God to move in His perfect timing. Keep in mind that if you don't ask God for anything, you won't receive anything. You can't be upset with Him if things aren't going well in your life if you haven't given Him full access to you. Commune with our Father in Heaven expecting to have what you've asked for according to His will. Your life changes tremendously when you spend time with God daily.

SEPTEMBER 24ᵀᴴ

Take Every Thought Captive

———◆———

"We demolish arguments and every pretension that sets itself up against the knowledge of God, and we take captive every thought to make it obedient to Christ." 2 Corinthians 10:5 (NIV)

Negative thoughts will enter your mind at times bringing you into a dark place, but you have to cast down those thoughts. The devil will make you think about things that haven't happened yet to take you out of the present moment. This is how he steals your peace and joy. When the devil distracts you with worry about future events, use the authority God gave you and tell Satan to go. Tell him, "Nope not today Satan." Bring yourself back into the present moment and enjoy the gift of today that God has graciously given you. He has blessed you with another day to do great things.

SEPTEMBER 25ᵀᴴ

Forgiven and Purified

"If we claim to be without sin, we deceive ourselves and the truth is not in us. If we confess our sins, He is faithful and just and will forgive us our sins and purify us from all unrighteousness." 1 John 1:8-9 (NIV)

As human beings, we all have sinned. None of us are perfect. We are a work in progress. It takes time to grow into the person God created us to be. You will make mistakes from time to time, but confess your sin and God will forgive you. Don't worry about what others may say. Once you confess your sins to God, He will forgive you. He gives you a clean slate to start again. He loves you and He wants to purify you, then He can use you to do great works. Keep going as you become stronger and wiser.

SEPTEMBER 26ᵀᴴ

Don't Judge God's Servants

———◆◆◆———

"Who art thou that judgest another man's servant? To his own master he standeth or falleth. Yea, he shall be holden up: for God is able to make him stand." Romans 14:4 (KJV)

God's children are His servants. We serve others here on earth as the Lord guides us. Although you are made righteous through Christ, you may stumble at times. Remember that you have also made mistakes if you see your brother or sister fall. Don't judge them if they fall. Do your part by encouraging them to get back up. They are God's children, not yours to judge. You can't make them stand up when they fall, but you can be an ear for them and also encouragement for them. If you fall and God helps you back up, turn around to help your neighbor up when they fall.

SEPTEMBER 27ᵀᴴ

Build Up Your Neighbor

"Each of us should please our neighbors for their good, to build them up. For even Christ did not please Himself but, as it is written: 'The insults of those who insult you have fallen on Me." Romans 15:2-3 (NIV)

Jesus takes on your suffering. When people hurt you, remember that Christ was hurt first. He will teach you how to endure the harder times. He suffered great pain to show you how to be a conqueror over your own pain. He loves you very much and encourages you through His Word. You should be a lot more like Christ and encourage the people God brings into your life. We need to build others up so we can become more unified and stronger together. Put your own needs aside sometimes and help meet someone else's needs. Make it your goal to help at least one person everyday.

SEPTEMBER 28TH

Avoid Bitterness

———◆———

"See to it that no one falls short of the grace of God and that no bitter root grows up to cause trouble and defile many."
Hebrews 12:15 (NIV)

We are God's chosen people. We have to be great examples for those around us to show them how God's children should carry themselves. We are who God has chosen to lead others and it is our job to lead them the right way. You cannot let someone's bitterness cause issues such as division among the people. Keep yourself from falling into any kind of drama or trouble so that the devil cannot take foothold. If something happens between you and someone else, quickly resolve the issue allowing you to keep a spirit of peace among you all. Love your brothers and sisters with all you have. Love them with the love of Jesus.

Instructions Every Morning

"The Sovereign Lord has given me a well-instructed tongue, to know the Word that sustains the weary. He wakens me morning by morning, wakens my ear to listen like one being instructed." Isaiah 50:4 (NIV)

Waking up in the morning gets easier to do when you know you're waking to the Lord's Word. His Word gives you peace and joy. It energizes your spirit. Give the Lord your requests for the day. Then take some time in the morning before you start the day to read His Word. When you give the Lord your time, He will give Himself back to you. He will instruct your tongue when you are speaking with people, giving you the right words to strengthen and encourage them. You will hear His voice as you spend time in His Word. More Word equals more guidance through the Holy Spirit.

SEPTEMBER 30TH

God Doesn't Tempt Us

"When tempted, no one should say, 'God is tempting me.' For God cannot be tempted by evil, nor does He tempt anyone; but each person is tempted when they are dragged away by their own evil desire and enticed." James 1:13-14 (NIV)

God doesn't tempt His children. He allows Satan to tempt you in order to refine you. Satan will use your own desires to entice you. This is how you grow stronger in your faith. You learn how to depend on God even more as you face temptation. Be aware of the different ways Satan will tempt you. Satan uses people you love, your thoughts, or things to tempt you. Although temptation can feel overwhelming, remember in the midst of tests that it's an opportunity to become stronger in Christ. It's also the gateway to the next level in your life. Stand strong.

Hear the Word, Do the Word

"But whoever looks intently into the perfect law that gives freedom, and continues in it - not forgetting what they have heard, but doing it - they will be blessed in what they do."
James 1:25 (NIV)

Reading God's Word is a good start to a great transformation in your life, but it's not enough to be a hearer of His Word. If you want to see a great change in your life, you must also be a doer of His Word. This is where you will experience great freedom. Read God's Word daily and put it into practice. When you see how much your life changes and how free you feel, you won't be able to get enough of God's Word. Your life will be overflowed with love, light, perfect peace, and joy. Read, listen, and then do what God's Word says. You will be blessed in all that you do.

You Are A Victor

———◆◆◆———

"To him that overcometh will I grant to sit with Me in My throne, even as I also overcame, and am sat down with My Father in His throne." Revelation 3:21 (KJV)

Jesus was victorious over death and is now sitting down with our Heavenly Father. Jesus invites the ones who are victorious to come and sit with Him on the throne. Continue to be a warrior and a conqueror in the Kingdom. We always look at the mountains ahead of us and think it's too hard to climb, but we forget about the mountains behind us that we've already climbed. God is with you as you climb every mountain and if you remain in Him, you will make it over every single one. You are victorious through Christ and will one day sit with Him on the throne. You are a victor.

Love All People

"Suppose a man comes into your meeting wearing a gold ring and fine clothes, and a poor man in filthy old clothes also comes in. If you show special attention to the man wearing fine clothes and say, 'Here's a good seat for you,' but say to the poor man, 'You stand there' or 'Sit on the floor by my feet,' have you not discriminated among yourselves and become judges with evil thoughts?" James 2:2-4 (NIV)

God wants you to treat everyone the same. Don't treat someone who's rich better than someone who's poor. Jesus is a King, but He didn't come here as a King. Jesus helped all people. We entertain angels unknowingly. Remember that the next time someone needs your help. It could be a test to see how you treat people. The person may be an angel in disguise. Help all people.

Empathize With Others

———◦◦———

"Rejoice with them that do rejoice; and weep with them that weep. Be of the same mind one toward another. Mind not high things, but condescend to men of low estate. Be not wise in your own conceits." Romans 12:15-16 (KJV)

Have empathy for one another. Be careful not to judge someone else if you haven't sat where they've sat. Try to understand what they are going through and help lift them up from their low place. If you become too high-minded or conceited, God will humble you so you can be touched by the feeling of someone else's infirmities. Even God wrapped Himself up in flesh so that He could sit where we sit understanding our physical and mental weaknesses in order to help free us. Lower yourself in position in order to help lift up your brother or sister to a higher position.

Not By Might Nor By Power

———◆◆———

"So he said to me, 'This is the word of the Lord to Zerubbabel: 'Not by might nor by power, but by My Spirit,' says the Lord Almighty." Zechariah 4:6 (NIV)

Allow the Lord to guide your steps. Everyday before you go out into the world, ask the Holy Spirit to lead and guide you. There are things that may be too hard for you to accomplish in your own power. If you do things in your own power, you will eventually tire out and become exhausted. When you're exhausted, you're no good to anybody including yourself. The Holy Spirit gives you the power, strength, energy, the right thoughts, and words to do great things for God's Kingdom. Do all things through the power of the Holy Spirit. Let go of your own will and allow God's will to be done. His will is perfect.

OCTOBER 6TH

A Future Hope For You

"Do not let your heart envy sinners, but always be zealous for the fear of the Lord. There is surely a future hope for you, and your hope will not be cut off." Proverbs 23:17-18 (NIV)

There is no reason to be jealous of a sinner. At times you wonder why you have to deal with the consequences of your sin while they're still having a good time without all the troubles for their sins. It seems like they do whatever they want and get away with it, but that's not your business. You can't get away with the same things, but that's because you are God's child. You have a future hope and God will allow you to suffer until you learn to do things His way. Get excited because you will not be cut off from what God has planned for you. You are His.

OCTOBER 7TH

Love With Actions and in Truth

———◆———

"Dear children, let us not love with words or speech but with actions and in truth. This is how we know that we belong to the truth and how we set our hearts at rest in His presence: If our hearts condemn us, we know that God is greater than our hearts, and He knows everything." 1 John 3:18-20 (NIV)

Anyone can say they love someone and want to help, but what are your actions saying? Do you actually go and help the person or just say it? If you help your brother or sister and still feel like you aren't doing enough for them, your heart condemns you. You feel like what you've done for them isn't good enough, but God knows your true motives and He's so much greater than your conscience. Keep working hard for the Lord while loving others with your actions, not just words.

OCTOBER 8TH

Ask For What You Want

"What do you want me to do for you?" Jesus asked him. The blind man said, 'Rabbi, I want to see." Mark 10:51 (NIV)

Jesus will answer your prayers according to His will. You have to ask Him for whatever it is that you want. God will open your eyes allowing you to see. He will open your ears allowing you to hear. God loves to bless His children. He loves to give you the desires of your heart according to His will. When God opens your eyes and ears, you will start to see Him everywhere. You will hear His voice through different things or people. The more you study and meditate on His Word, the more you will notice Him around you. He's right there guiding your steps and lighting the way for your feet. Ask Him to let you see and hear Him. Your life will change forever.

God Chose You

———❖———

"You did not choose Me, but I chose you and appointed you so that you might go and bear fruit - fruit that will last - and so that whatever you ask in My name the Father will give you." John 15:16 (NIV)

We sometimes forget that we were chosen by God. We think we chose Him, but He formed us for a specific purpose before the foundation of the world. He chose us to do great works that will continue on for generations. You have to realize your true value and worth. Ask God to reveal your true purpose. He has a specific mission that only you can accomplish, but you won't fulfill it without His help. Ask for whatever you need in Jesus' name and our Heavenly Father will provide it in order to complete His will for your life.

OCTOBER 10TH

Pray in Faith

———◆———

"And the prayer offered in faith will make the sick person well; the Lord will raise them up. If they have sinned, they will be forgiven." James 5:15 (NIV)

Everyone has something they struggle with in life. None of us have it all together, but that's why Jesus died. He gave His life to free you from whatever holds you captive. We all have different devils we're fighting. Some of us fight daily against our captor. Your faith is what makes you whole. Your freedom and salvation is Jesus. He raises the dead and heals the sick. He forgives your sins and makes you new. Being saved does not mean you're going to be perfect. It's a lifelong process. God forgives your sins and He is cleansing you one day at a time. Enjoy the process and experience real freedom. Pray with faith.

OCTOBER 11TH

Revealing Our Destiny

"Dear friends, now we are children of God, and what we will be has not yet been made known. But we know that when Christ appears, we shall be like Him, for we shall see Him as He is." 1 John 3:2 (NIV)

Every single one of us is on a journey to become better people, to become more like Jesus. On your journey, you will go through experiences. Some of them will be painful and some will be joyous. Each experience will bring out new characteristics and skills you didn't know you had. God hides your destiny within you and as you take another step forward, you will continue blossoming into what He created you to be. Even when you're afraid to go on, push past your fear and take another step. Do it scared, do it anyway and you will begin walking in your purpose. You will shine.

OCTOBER 12TH

Shine Among Them

"Do everything without grumbling or arguing, so that you may become blameless and pure, 'children of God without fault in a warped and crooked generation.' Then you will shine among them like the stars in the sky as you hold firmly to the Word of life. And then I will be able to boast on the day of Christ that I did not run or labor in vain." Philippians 2:14-16 (NIV)

God chose you to be a light in a dark world. He uses you as an example of how God's children should carry themselves. The world is dark enough right now with all that is going on. You can't stop what's going on, but you can make the places God puts you in a little brighter. You can do your part by helping change the world one person at a time. Sometimes just smiling at someone can brighten their day.

OCTOBER 13TH

I Will Not Be Shaken

"Yes, my soul, find rest in God; my hope comes from Him. Truly He is my rock and my salvation; He is my fortress, I will not be shaken." Psalm 62:5-6 (NIV)

All kinds of troubles may rise up at different moments in your life. It can be very stressful. When waves rise up to overtake you, they won't be able to because you are God's child. The wind may blow, but you will not be moved. God is your rock and your refuge. He will not allow anything to move you from your spot until He decides to move you into something better. When God has His hand on you, there is no devil that can destroy you. God will finish what He started in you. When your enemies come up against you, they will not have victory over you. Rest easy in His arms knowing He is keeping you from drowning.

OCTOBER 14TH

All-Surpassing Power

———◆———

"But we have this treasure in jars of clay to show that this all-surpassing power is from God and not from us. We are hard pressed on every side, but not crushed; perplexed, but not in despair; persecuted, but not abandoned; struck down, but not destroyed." 2 Corinthians 4:7-9 (NIV)

Whenever you're feeling defeated, turn to God for help. There will be bumps in the road, but it doesn't mean you're losing. Storms will eventually come. They come to teach you to depend on God. Reach out to Him and remember that all things are possible with Him. God will allow you to suffer to remind you that you can do nothing apart from Him. The moment you become too comfortable doing things in your own power, God will show you how weak you really are. Allow God's power to work through you.

Consider It Pure Joy

"Consider it pure joy, my brothers and sisters, whenever you face trials of many kinds, because you know that the testing of your faith produces perseverance. Let perseverance finish its work so that you may be mature and complete, not lacking anything." James 1:2-4 (NIV)

You grow wiser and more mature as you climb the mountains ahead of you. As trials come to test you, hold on to your faith and your joy remembering that this too shall pass. Learn from the difficult times instead of going around the same mountain over and over again. These trials produce faith, making you whole. As you continue on your journey, the test that come are important because it's how you grow. Keep growing into the person God intended for you to be. Stay persistent in your walk with God.

You Are Forgiven

——◆——

"Therefore, I tell you, her many sins have been forgiven - as her great love has shown. But whoever has been forgiven little loves little." Luke 7:47 (NIV)

No one is perfect. We all make mistakes at times. If you mess up, ask for forgiveness and continue walking on the path God has blessed you to walk. Jesus took on our sins so that we could be free and have a relationship with our Heavenly Father. If God gave His Son for you and forgives you for your sins, then why shouldn't you also forgive others for their mistakes. The depth of your forgiveness will determine the depth of your love. Those who have the most powerful and the greatest love are those who have been forgiven greatly.

OCTOBER 17TH

Running The Race

"Therefore, since we are surrounded by such a great cloud of witnesses, let us throw off everything that hinders and the sin that so easily entangles. And let us run with perseverance the race marked out for us, fixing our eyes on Jesus, the pioneer and perfecter of faith. For the joy set before Him He endured the cross, scorning its shame, and sat down at the right hand of the throne of God." Hebrews 12:1-2 (NIV)

There will be stumbling blocks along the way on your journey to greatness, but God will not allow you to fall. He will keep you. Do not allow sin to take over completely. If you stumble, quickly get back on track and run the race God has given you to run. Your finish line is at the right hand of the throne of God.

God's Face Shines On You

"The Lord bless you and keep you; the Lord make His face shine on you and be gracious to you; the Lord turn His face toward you and give you peace." Numbers 6:24-26 (NIV)

Jesus is your protector. He won't let anything take you down. He pours out His grace over you whenever you're feeling overwhelmed or unsure. His light shines brightly through you and around you when you're going through dark times in your life. He's the light for your feet allowing you to see your way on the path He's blessed you to walk daily. His eyes are focused on you everyday as you follow Him to every new level in your life, growing into the person you were destined to be. As you follow Him, He blesses you with perfect peace and you know deep down in your heart, He won't allow you to lose.

You Don't Have To Worry

"Then Jesus said to His disciples: 'Therefore I tell you, do not worry about your life, what you will eat; or about your body, what you will wear. For life is more than food, and the body more than clothes." Luke 12:22-23 (NIV)

Stay seated at the feet of Jesus. Your seat is your position of authority over Satan. If Satan can get you to worry about things like what you're going to eat, wear, or where you will live, then he can take you out of the power Jesus has given you over him. You have to remain in your seat of authority and use the power Jesus gives you over the enemy. Remain in perfect peace knowing that if God feeds the animals who don't work, why wouldn't He feed you? As the bible says, 'Are you not much more valuable than they?' DO NOT WORRY.

You Will Not Stay In Darkness

"Then Jesus cried out, 'Whoever believes in Me does not believe in Me only, but in the One who sent Me. The one who looks at Me is seeing the One who sent Me. I have come into the world as a light, so that no one who believes in Me should stay in darkness." John 12:44-46 (NIV)

Jesus is God in the flesh. God came in the flesh to teach us His ways, His truth, and to be our guiding light. Life can get dark at times, but Jesus is your light. He fills your life with light and He allows you to see your way out of darkness. When you are saved, dark times will still come, but you won't stay in the dark. God will brighten up the darker days and will guide you out of them through His Holy Spirit. Fear not because God's children will never be left alone in the dark.

OCTOBER 21ST

God Has The Power

———•◆•———

"Yet he did not waver through unbelief regarding the promise of God, but was strengthened in his faith and gave glory to God, being fully persuaded that God had power to do what He had promised." Romans 4:20-21 (NIV)

We walk by faith, not by sight. When things are not looking the way you hoped they would, keep trusting that God will do what He promised you. God will not break His promise to you. God is preparing you for the blessing He already has waiting for you. Sometimes your character needs to be developed more before you can receive the blessing God has for you. Be patient and wait for God's perfect timing knowing that God won't break His promises or His Word. Continue trusting God completely no matter what things look like. He won't let you down.

OCTOBER 22ND

Your Faith Is Pleasing To God

"And without faith it is impossible to please God, because anyone who comes to Him must believe that He exists and that He rewards those who earnestly seek Him." Hebrews 11:6 (NIV)

When you begin feeling fear about the next level in your life, continue on in faith. Don't allow fear to run your life. It's actually quite simple, you either trust Him or you don't. God loves when you walk toward His promises with confidence. Go after everything He has for you with your all. Believe God in every situation, even the ones which seem impossible. He will reward you with blessings as you continue on your path, believing He will make you into what He has created you to be. Keep walking by faith and He will do the molding. He will turn your mess into a masterpiece. Trust Him fully.

God Is Establishing Your Goings

"I waited patiently for the Lord; and He inclined unto me, and heard my cry. He brought me up also out of a horrible pit, out of the miry clay, and set my feet upon a rock, and established my goings." Psalm 40:1-2 (KJV)

There will be times you feel like giving up. You feel like you've fought and fought, but it hasn't gotten you anywhere. The Lord will not put more on you than you can handle. Be patient, trust God's perfect plan. He has not forgotten about you. He hears your cries and He will pick you up out of any darkness. He will lift you up and set you on a rock. He will guide you and keep you as you go after your calling. Don't worry about anything. If God makes you wait a little while, it doesn't mean He's telling you no. He is preparing you for your blessing.

The Path Of Life

———◆———

"You make known to me the path of life; You will fill me with joy in Your presence, with eternal pleasures at Your right hand." Psalm 16:11 (NIV)

As you follow Jesus, He will open doors for you and guide you toward the best life you could ever have. It is a fight though, but He will strengthen you for the fight as He overflows you with the greatest joy you'll ever experience. He will overflow you with love and perfect peace as you follow Him through the doors He opens for you, guiding you toward the path of life. When you first enter a new level, it will feel a little strange, but continue to follow Him as He molds you into the person He created you to be. Fight against the gravity trying to pull you back down. Don't allow any fear to stop you from His promises.

The Lord Is My Shepherd

"The Lord is my shepherd, I lack nothing. He makes me lie down in green pastures, He leads me beside quiet waters, He refreshes my soul. He guides me along the right paths for His name's sake." Psalm 23:1-3 (NIV)

When you allow Jesus to guide you, He will provide you with everything you need. You may not always get what you want, but He will always give you what you need. The Lord will allow you to relax in perfect peace. As you sit still and quiet your mind, the Lord will allow you to hear Him as He instructs you along the right path. If you stray from the path, don't give up completely. Quickly return to Him and He will continue to guide you in the right direction. He wants to use you for His glory, don't be afraid of your destiny.

OCTOBER 26TH

Believe God's Faithfulness

———◦◆◦———

"And by faith even Sarah, who was past childbearing age, was enabled to bear children because she considered Him faithful who had made the promise." Hebrews 11:11 (NIV)

God doesn't bless you based on age. He blesses you based on stage. It doesn't matter how young or old you are when God has something for you. Your faith is what pleases God and if you trust God, He will strengthen you for His promises. When you are getting ready to receive what God promised you, it won't be easy. Things will get very difficult first in your life. Be determined in your spirit that no matter what obstacles come, you will not lay down and die. Get ready to receive what God has promised you, but keep in mind that it will be a fight. Keep fighting. God didn't bring you this far to leave you.

OCTOBER 27ᵀᴴ

More Mature And Complete

———◆———

"Let perseverance finish its work so that you may be mature and complete, not lacking anything." James 1:4 (NIV)

Following Jesus wherever He wants you to go is not easy. It definitely gets difficult at times, but those times are necessary for you to grow into who God created you to be. Plants grow from the rain and the sunlight. We're no different. You need both the rainy days and the brighter days to mature into your calling. Jesus will take you on a journey with Him, but be prepared to endure the bumps in the road along the way. Pain doesn't feel good, but it's how you learn and mature. He is maturing you into who He called you to be. Continue to stay close to Him even when things get tough. He won't leave you to do life alone. Trust Him even when you're not sure.

OCTOBER 28TH

The Lord's Instruction

"I will instruct you and teach you in the way you should go; I will counsel you with My loving eye on you." Psalm 32:8 (NIV)

On your journey toward destiny, you will come to points in your life where you have to make tough decisions. Ask the Lord which path you should take. Be willing to hear the counsel of Jesus. He will speak to you through people or things, but be sure to test the spirits as they speak to you. Be sure that it is the Lord's counsel that you are following. The Lord watches over you with love and He wants nothing but the best for you. As a child of the Most High, the King, you are destined for His best. Jesus will make a way out of no way for you and then you will know it had to be God who blessed you. Listen closely for your next instruction.

OCTOBER 29ᵀᴴ

Forgive As The Lord Forgives

"Bear with each other and forgive one another if any of you has a grievance against someone. Forgive as the Lord forgave you." Colossians 3:13 (NIV)

People will hurt you at some point in your life. They may hurt you directly or indirectly, but either way it doesn't feel good. When you experience hurt, don't hold onto it. If you hold on to how someone hurt you, it will only cause you to be bitter. Bitterness can take over you completely and in the end, it will only hurt you. The next time someone hurts you, forgive them. It won't be easy, but think about how many times the Lord has forgiven you whenever you have made mistakes. You will get back whatever you give out. If you expect God's grace and forgiveness for your mistakes, give others the same grace. Forgive them.

OCTOBER 30TH

Sharpen Others

———◆———

"As iron sharpens iron, so one person sharpens another."
Proverbs 27:17 (NIV)

It's always a blessing to have a good team around you. True friends and family will be there for you when things aren't pretty. They won't leave you when things get rough. Real family and friends will be honest with you. They won't agree with everything you do. They will tell you what you need to hear, not what you want to hear. It's important to have a good team around you that will help you be the best person you can be. You are truly blessed when you can count on your friends and family to extend a hand. They're the ones who help you regain focus when you lose sight of your goals. Don't take your loved ones for granted. Love them while you have the chance. They won't be here forever.

OCTOBER 31ˢᵀ

Transformation

———◦◦———

"And we all, who with unveiled faces contemplate the Lord's glory, are being transformed into His image with ever-increasing glory, which comes from the Lord, who is the Spirit." 2 Corinthians 3:18 (NIV)

Walking with the Lord is beautiful and it feels amazing. You begin to transform into this beautiful person. Your spirit begins to become one with the Lord's. He places new desires in your heart and gives you the passion to go after those desires. You are like a baby when you first give your life to Christ. First you crawl, then you walk, and eventually run in the promises of God. As you run after His promises, He blesses you with wings to soar into your destiny. All the suffering you experienced will be worth the glory that is revealed in you as you transform.

NOVEMBER 1ST

The Lord's Covenant

———◆———

"Sovereign Lord, You are God. Your covenant is trustworthy, and You have promised these good things to Your servant." 2 Samuel 7:28 (NIV)

God has a special agreement with His children. He blesses us with great promises that He will not break. The further you walk with the Lord, the more you realize how trustworthy He is. You start to feel a peace which surpasses all understanding, realizing that all things work together for the good of those who walk with the Lord and are called according to His purpose. God always makes a way for you, leading you to victory. Trust is power. Walk with the Lord through everything and trust that you can lean on Him the whole way through your journey. Life becomes a lot easier to enjoy whenever you let go and give God all power over your life.

NOVEMBER 2ND

The Good News

❖

"We tell you the good news: What God promised our ancestors, He has fulfilled for us, their children, by raising up Jesus. As it is written in the second Psalm: 'You are My Son; today I have become Your Father.' God raised Him from the dead so that He will never be subject to decay. As God has said, 'I will give you the holy and sure blessings promised to David."
Acts 13:32-34 (NIV)

God kept His promise by raising up Jesus, who conquered death. You have the same power that raised Jesus from the dead within you. You are given power through the Holy Spirit to conquer death. You are now alive in Christ, free from a life of misery. God has raised you up. You have His power living within you. He has given you authority over darkness so use it. You will live and not die.

NOVEMBER 3RD

Your Deliverance

—◆—

"Moses answered the people, 'Do not be afraid. Stand firm and you will see the deliverance the Lord will bring you today. The Egyptians you see today you will never see again. The Lord will fight for you; you need only to be still." Exodus 14:13-14 (NIV)

Storms will rise up in your life. When they come, it feels like Satan is only attacking you, but you have nothing to fear. The Lord is keeping you. Continue to stand strong through these test knowing that God won't let you fall. When the enemy comes against you, be still. Don't allow your circumstances to take your peace. Your peace will allow you to think more clearly. When you lose your peace, you allow Satan to control your next move. Stay calm, be still and let the Lord fight for you. He will win you the victory.

NOVEMBER 4ᵀᴴ

God Chooses Who He Wants

"Who will bring any charge against those whom God has chosen? It is God who justifies. Who then is the one who condemns? No one. Christ Jesus who died - more than that, who was raised to life - is at the right hand of God and is also interceding for us." Romans 8:33-34 (NIV)

God chooses whomever He wants regardless of what others think or feel. He's the One who molds you into the person He needs you to be to use you for His glory. When you're chosen by God, it isn't about you. He's using you to bring others out of bondage. Remain humble as God uses you to help His people. Jesus conquered death and His Spirit intercedes for you. He's guiding you and is teaching you through His Holy Spirit. Be open to learning what God's purpose is for you. He chose you for something great.

308

NOVEMBER 5TH

Strength and Peace

———◆———

"The Lord will give strength unto His people; the Lord will bless His people with peace." Psalm 29:11 (KJV)

When God calls you to do something great for His Kingdom, it may seem like an impossible task. Be sure that it won't always be easy, but follow Him taking one step at a time. He will strengthen you as you continue walking toward your purpose. He will bless you with all you need to do what He's called you to do. The journey will get a little tough at times, but He will bless you with peace even in the tougher times. Keep your mind focused on Jesus and not the task. Trust that He will lead you in all situations, but you have to let go and allow God to work through you. Keep walking by faith as He transforms you into what He's called you to be in His Heavenly Kingdom.

God Of All Grace

———◆◆◆———

"And the God of all grace, who called you to His eternal glory in Christ, after you have suffered a little while, will Himself restore you and make you strong, firm and steadfast." 1 Peter 5:10 (NIV)

Before God can use you in a mighty way, you have to be molded. You are being fitted for the position God has for you in His Kingdom. You will go through both good days and dark days. You will need them both to grow. Growing is always uncomfortable. While you are suffering, it's easy to ask God questions like, "Why me God?" But the question to you is, "Why not you?" Whoever can endure suffering for awhile are the blessed and chosen children of God. Hold on to God tightly. This too shall pass and when it does, God will restore you. He will make you strong for your purpose.

Don't Be Afraid Of People

"Do not be afraid of those who can kill the body but cannot kill the soul. Rather, be afraid of the One who can destroy both soul and body in Hell." Matthew 10:28 (NIV)

God didn't give you the spirit of fear. He gave you the spirit of love and power. Don't be afraid to tell people who your God is and what He's done in your life. None of those people can kill your soul or take your position in Heaven away from you, but God can. He can destroy your soul and body. Listen to His instructions and allow Him to use you. People can laugh at you, call you names, and even kill your body, but they can never stop you from getting into Heaven. Let God guide your actions and not people. He is the one who will save you in the end. Be wise and accept your royal position in the Kingdom.

NOVEMBER 8TH

Build A Good Team

"When Moses' hands grew tired, they took a stone and put it under him and he sat on it. Aaron and Hur held his hands up - one on one side, one on the other - so that his hands remained steady till sunset." Exodus 17:12 (NIV)

It is good to have people around you that will help hold you up whenever you feel like you can't go on any longer. Make sure you have a dependable team of people you can trust who will have your back through anything. It's equally important to be a person your team can trust to hold them up in the same way if they are feeling weak. Be the person to them that you want them to be to you. When you have strong faith in God and a strong team, whether it be friends or family, you can accomplish the impossible.

It Is More Blessed To Give

———◆———

"In everything I did, I showed you that by this kind of hard work we must help the weak, remembering the words the Lord Jesus Himself said: 'It is more blessed to give than to receive."
Acts 20:35 (NIV)

God will bless you with opportunities to help others who are weak. He will use you to help strengthen others. He overflows you with an abundance of love, joy, peace, and wisdom until it spills out over into the lives of those He has placed in your life. God will bless you with prosperity in all areas of your life, but it's not just for you. He blesses you because He trusts you to bless others. Jesus makes it clear that the ones who give are the ones who are more blessed. The more you bless others, the more God will bless you. Be giving to those who are in need.

Counted As Blessed

"As you know, we count as blessed those who have persevered. You have heard of Job's perseverance and have seen what the Lord finally brought about. The Lord is full of compassion and mercy." James 5:11 (NIV)

Job from the bible was very faithful to God. Even when he lost his whole family and everything, he remained faithful. He trusted God no matter how bad things looked. In the end, God blessed Job with more than he had before because of his faithfulness. You will also be tested in your life. Trust God even when it feels like you're losing everything. Remain faithful and God will overflow you with more than you lost. Your circumstances may not look the way you'd hoped, but trust that God will exalt you in His perfect timing. Get ready for double blessings.

NOVEMBER 11ᵀᴴ

Take Negative Thoughts Captive

"We demolish arguments and every pretension that sets itself up against the knowledge of God, and we take captive every thought to make it obedient to Christ." 2 Corinthians 10:5 (NIV)

While following Christ, you'll experience spiritual warfare. The war begins in the mind. Satan will put negative, fearful, and dark thoughts in your mind as often as he can. It's important to cast these thoughts down as soon as they start. People mistake these thoughts as their own and allow them to grow until the thoughts control their actions. Don't allow the enemy to trick you. These thoughts are not your thoughts. Take authority over negative thoughts. Fill your life with positive people. Fill your mind and spirit with positivity. Allow love to be the driving force in your life, not fear.

Chosen To See God

⬥◆⬥

"Then he said: 'The God of our ancestors has chosen you to know His will and to see the Righteous One and to hear words from His mouth. You will be His witness to all people of what you have seen and heard. And now what are you waiting for? Get up, be baptized and wash your sins away, calling on His name." Acts 22:14-16 (NIV)

God comes along when you least expect it. He chooses you to see Him and hear Him. He chooses the most messed up people, then He cleans them up so that people will see His glory and His power. No one can deny the power of God when they see the transformation of a sinner. You've been chosen by God. Welcome to the Royal Family. He's getting ready to use you in a mighty way for the glory of His Kingdom. Congratulations on being chosen by the Most High.

NOVEMBER 13TH

My cup overflows

———◆———

"You prepare a table before me in the presence of my enemies. You anoint my head with oil; my cup overflows." Psalm 23:5 (NIV)

God blesses His children with abundance. He loves to bless us with great gifts. Although none of us deserve anything, God still overflows us with more than we could ever dream of as we continue on the path He has blessed us to walk. Always remember to bless others the way God is blessing you. He gives an abundance to those He can trust will use it to the benefit of the Kingdom. The more grateful and giving you are, the more God will overflow you with blessings. Be open-handed toward your brothers and sisters. When God is your main resource, you will never go without.

Being Used By God

————◆◆————

"I, the Lord, have called you in righteousness; I will take hold of your hand. I will keep you and will make you to be a covenant for the people and a light for the gentiles, to open eyes that are blind, to free captives from prison and to release from the dungeon those who sit in darkness." Isaiah 42:6-7 (NIV)

God has called you to Himself and He is molding you into the person He has created you to be. All the suffering you are going through is necessary to grow you into a stronger and wiser child of God. He chose you to come into agreement with Him so that He could grow you and then use you to free more of His children who are trapped in darkness. He has given you a great testimony and it's up to you to use it as a key to someone else's freedom. Choose to be a light.

You Are Radiant Through Christ

"They looked unto Him, and were lightened: and their faces were not ashamed." Psalm 34:5 (KJV)

On your journey toward greatness, there will be little bumps in the road that will come. When the rougher times come, use it as an opportunity to depend on the Lord even more. Hold on to Him tighter. Allow God to lead the way. Allow His thoughts to become intertwined with your thoughts. Move the way God would move resisting your old ways of thinking. Your light will shine brighter as you allow God's Spirit to move through you. The closer you get to God, the easier it gets to resist the devil's traps when they come. God won't allow you to be covered in shame. He will protect you from the tricks of the enemy. Be grateful for the protective shield God has over you.

Jesus Has Already Overcome

———◆———

"I have told you these things, so that in Me you may have peace. In this world you will have trouble. But take heart. I have overcome the world." John 16:33 (NIV)

Open yourself up to hearing God's voice. Allow the Holy Spirit to lead you throughout the day. Following Jesus allows you to have perfect peace even when trouble comes. Don't fight in the flesh, fight in the spirit. It helps to remember that Jesus has already won the war. He already defeated the enemy. If you focus on Jesus when troubles rise up, He will fight the battle for you. The best thing you can do during a trial is to pray and be still. You don't have to fight your battles alone because you have God on your side and He will not allow you to lose. Remain in peace and trust God to fight for you.

NOVEMBER 17ᵀᴴ

Now Get Up And Witness

———◆◆———

"Now get up and stand on your feet. I have appeared to you to appoint you as a servant and as a witness of what you have seen and will see of Me. I will rescue you from your own people and from the Gentiles. I am sending you to them to open their eyes and turn them from darkness to light, and from the power of Satan to God, so that they may receive forgiveness of sins and a place among those who are sanctified by faith in Me."
Acts 26:16-18 (NIV)

Being chosen by God can be scary at times. It doesn't feel great at first. When He chooses you, He cleans you up first. The process can get hard, but trust God's way. He is strengthening you to be a soldier in the war between good and evil. He's using you to bring His children out of Satan's grip. Keep your eyes on Him.

You Lack Nothing

"The Lord is my Shepherd, I lack nothing. He makes me lie down in green pastures, He leads me beside quiet waters, He refreshes my soul. He guides me along the right paths for His name's sake." Psalm 23:1-3 (NIV)

When you allow Jesus to be your guide, He will make sure you have all you need along the way. Although His way is the best way, you will experience tough times as well, but He will give you perfect peace in these times. Your soul will be refreshed and your spirit will be strengthened through God's Word. Allow His Word to fill you up and transform you completely from the inside out. God is strengthening your inner man for the journey ahead of you.

Let Go Of Control

———◆◆◆———

"Do not be anxious about anything, but in every situation, by prayer and petition, with thanksgiving, present your requests to God. And the peace of God, which transcends all understanding, will guard your hearts and your minds in Christ Jesus." Philippians 4:6-7 (NIV)

As human beings we tend to try and control everything. We want things to go the way we think they should go, but that's impossible. We can't control the actions of others or the outcomes of every situation. We can only control ourselves. Allowing God to be God blesses your spirit with great peace. Pray to God in everything, but be willing to accept God's will for your life. Be grateful to God for whatever the outcome is. God loves you. He wants to give you a great ending here on earth so let Him.

We Are Being Guided Home

———◆◆◆———

"In Your unfailing love You will lead the people You have redeemed. In Your strength You will guide them to Your holy dwelling." Exodus 15:13 (NIV)

God's love for you is unconditional. He loves you no matter what you do. Jesus came to save you from a life of darkness and sin. He will meet you wherever you are in your life. He reveals Himself to whomever He chooses. After He saves you from darkness, He becomes the light for your feet. He lights the way ahead of you and leads you down the narrow path. He will continue to guide you home, showing you the way to His holy dwelling with the rest of the Royal Family. Don't stray away from the path, but if you do, quickly return to Him. Stay close to Him. Follow Him home.

NOVEMBER 21ST

Protected From Snakes

"But Paul shook the snake off into the fire and suffered no ill effects." Acts 28:5 (NIV)

Paul was bitten by a snake while getting closer to the fire, but because he had God protecting him, he shook it off and was not affected by it. When you're getting close to something great in your life, snakes will come out of nowhere to try and stop you. They come to keep you stuck in the same place you've always been. Pay attention when they come because it means you're closer than you've ever been to your blessing. If you're experiencing a lot of push-back in your life, it means your blessing is right on the other side. Hold on and get ready for your breakthrough to the next level. You will come out better than you were before without any ill effects just like Paul.

Ask, Believe, Receive

———◆———

"Truly I tell you, if anyone says to this mountain, 'Go, throw yourself into the sea,' and does not doubt in their heart but believes that what they say will happen, it will be done for them. Therefore I tell you, whatever you ask for in prayer, believe that you have received it, and it will be yours." Mark 11:23-24 (NIV)

There's power in your tongue. Whatever you speak will come to pass. That's why it's important to speak good things over your life and over the lives of others. Pray for whatever you're wanting, believing it's already yours. Thank God for whatever you're praying for because you have already received it. Pray for God's will over your life because He knows what's best for you. Wait patiently for God's perfect timing. Believe God for all things.

NOVEMBER 23RD

Knowledge To Escape

—————◆—————

"With their mouths the godless destroy their neighbors, but through knowledge the righteous escape." Proverbs 11:9 (NIV)

God chooses whomever He will. Being chosen isn't going to feel good all the time. When God begins to prosper you, people who you thought were your friends will start to become envious of you. They will start to speak negatively about you, but it's not your business what people say or think about you. They have free will just like you. If they want to hate you, they can. Don't allow that to affect the person God is molding you into. At the end of the day, God loves you no matter who likes it. Keep your eyes on Him and He will bless you with the knowledge to escape your enemies. He won't allow you to be destroyed by your haters. You are His, fear no man.

Jesus Is Coming

"Look, I am coming soon. My reward is with Me, and I will give to each person according to what they have done."
Revelation 22:12 (NIV)

The whole duty of man is to serve God. He blesses us with family and friends to accompany us while we're here on earth because He doesn't want any of us to be alone. He does this because He is a caring and loving God, but you can't lose focus on what He has called you to do. There is a time to work and a time to play. We don't know the exact time the Lord is coming, but don't be unprepared for His return. Work hard for Him in whatever He has called you to and you will be rewarded very greatly for it.

Rejoice, Pray, Give Thanks

—◆—

"Rejoice always, pray continually, give thanks in all circumstances; for this is God's will for you in Christ Jesus."
1 Thessalonians 5:16-18 (NIV)

God wants His children to be grateful in all circumstances in life, even in hardships. Being grateful in all circumstances will allow you to have a joy that cannot be taken from you. It is a joy which strengthens you and prepares you for anything that rises up in your life. Rejoice in everything, pray to our Lord continually, and be grateful for all outcomes. God prepares you for all things. Good times and hard times are essential ingredients for your growth. Be grateful, you need them both to mold you into the person God created you to be. Your gratitude is the secret to being successful in all areas of your life.

My Enemies Will Fall

———◆———

"When the wicked advance against me to devour me, it is my enemies and my foes who will stumble and fall. Though an army besiege me, my heart will not fear; though war break out against me, even then I will be confident." Psalm 27:2-3 (NIV)

God is transforming you daily. The enemy doesn't like that. The enemy sends people from your past to try and trap you in how they met you. They will call you "traitor" or "switch out". Don't get upset. People don't understand what they have never experienced. Remain focused and God will fight your battles. Your enemies will fall because God has you protected under the blood of Jesus. Continue moving forward in Christ remaining confident in your new transformation.

NOVEMBER 27TH

Live In The Present Moment

———◆———

"Therefore do not worry about tomorrow, for tomorrow will worry about itself. Each day has enough trouble of its own." Matthew 6:34 (NIV)

It's important to focus only on the step right in front of you. Don't worry about the next steps. Focus only on this step and things will begin to come together in God's perfect timing. Satan will send whatever he can to distract you. He will slow you down from reaching your destination by putting worrisome or fearful thoughts in your head. You can't change the future by worrying anyway so live in the present moment. You will experience full joy and peace when you practice being grateful for this very moment right now. When you're focused, you can accomplish anything. You will reach your full potential and achieve greatness.

Fullness In Christ

"I pray that out of His glorious riches He may strengthen you with power through His Spirit in your inner being, so that Christ may dwell in your hearts through faith. And I pray that you, being rooted and established in love, may have power, together with all the Lord's holy people, to grasp how wide and long and high and deep is the love of Christ, and to know this love of Christ, and to know this love that surpasses knowledge - that you may be filled to the measure of all the fullness of God." Ephesians 3:16-19 (NIV)

As you follow Christ, you are being strengthened in your faith. God is overflowing you with His love, blessing you with power through His Holy Spirit to fulfill all He has called you to. You're being transformed through the beauty of His love, wisdom, knowledge, and understanding.

Seek Good, Find Favor

———◆◆◆———

"He that diligently seeketh good procureth favour: but he that seeketh mischief, it shall come unto him." Proverbs 11:27 (KJV)

You get back whatever you put out. If you're doing evil or looking for it, that's what you'll get back. Go after good things such as God's Word. If you pursue God, He will pursue you. He will be the light that shines brightly through you and around you so that you can find your way through life. Others who are placed in your life will also see more clearly just by being around you because of the light that shines through you. As you continue following Christ, He will pour out His favor over your life. He is blessing you and your family with prosperity in all areas of your lives. Seek after your Heavenly Father daily. He will overflow you with blessings and His goodness.

New Compassion Every Morning

—◆—

"Because of the Lord's great love we are not consumed, for His compassions never fail. They are new every morning; great is Your faithfulness. I say to myself, 'The Lord is my portion; therefore I will wait for Him.' The Lord is good to those whose hope is in Him, to the one who seeks Him; it is good to wait quietly for the salvation of the Lord." Lamentations 3:22-26 (NIV)

It's a blessing to be broken by God. He breaks the old you, but He doesn't destroy you. He gracefully puts you back together. He is molding you into the new person He created you to be so that He can use you in a mighty way. He's such a forgiving and compassionate God. He allows you to start fresh every morning. He gives you the opportunity to turn your mess into a message. Remain faithful.

DECEMBER 1ST

Power Over Serpents

———◆———

"Behold, I give unto you power to tread on serpents and scorpions, and over all the power of the enemy: and nothing shall by any means hurt you." Luke 10:19 (KJV)

God does not leave His children powerless. He fills you with His power to overcome any obstacle the enemy has placed in your path to trip you up. When you're getting closer to your blessing, snakes will come out of nowhere to bite you. Do not be afraid of them. Use the power and authority God has given you to trample the head of the enemy. You may have been bitten, but you have not been beaten. God is all powerful while the enemy is powerless. You will overcome the enemy and you will win the victory.

DECEMBER 2ND

Counselled By God

"I will instruct thee and teach thee in the way which thou shalt go: I will guide thee with Mine eye." Psalm 32:8 (KJV)

You come to a point in your life where you grow tired of living the same old way. You begin to realize that your old ways aren't working for you. They aren't getting you anywhere. When you come to this realization, it's time to ask God for your next move. Ask Him to guide you and show you the way. He won't give it to you all at once, but one step at a time. God won't overwhelm you with too much. We usually do that to ourselves by trying to figure it all out in our flesh. Allow God to teach you and be your counselor. Since He created you, it only makes sense to ask Him what He created you for. Be patient and trust God fully through the process.

DECEMBER 3RD

Worship And Serve God Only

"Jesus said to him, 'Away from Me, Satan. For it is written: 'Worship the Lord your God, and serve Him only.' Then the devil left Him, and angels came and attended Him." Matthew 4:10-11 (NIV)

Jesus was led to the wilderness by the Spirit. He was tested by Satan for 40 days. Jesus resisted any temptation by the devil and eventually defeated him. After He defeated Satan, He started His ministry. It's important to remember that you too will experience your own kind of wilderness. You'll also be tested and tried before God can trust you with a ministry of your own. You'll experience many trials before God will bless you with a great ministry. If you're being tested, stay close to Jesus and He will teach you how to recognize the tricks of the enemy. He will show you how to defeat him.

Rebuilding And Restoring

"After this I will return and rebuild David's fallen tent. Its ruins I will rebuild, and I will restore it, that the rest of mankind may seek the Lord, even all the Gentiles who bear My name, says the Lord, who does these things things known from long ago." Acts 15:16-18 (NIV)

There will be times you want to lie down and die. Everything seems to be falling apart, but use this time as a turning point in your life. Now, you have a choice to make. You can choose to remain the same or choose to change. You can allow this obstacle to be a stumbling block or you can use this obstacle as a stepping stone to get up. If you allow the obstacle to be a stepping stone, God will rebuild and restore your life. He will use you to help others find their way by seeking Him.

DECEMBER 5TH

Straightening Your Path

———◆———

"Trust in the Lord with all your heart and lean not on your own understanding; in all your ways submit to Him, and He will make your paths straight." Proverbs 3:5-6 (NIV)

Being God's child is great, but it can also be difficult. God disciplines those He loves. He chose you to be a soldier in His Kingdom. He's training you daily. You're being strengthened and transformed through trials. Don't fight against what God is doing in your life. Learn from your mistakes and use it to your advantage. You won't always understand why you're going through certain battles, but it's not for you to understand. Don't question God. Trust Him fully. One day you'll look back and realize that it was good for you to be afflicted. It's made you stronger. Trust Him to lead you daily.

God Calls The Weak

———◆◆◆———

"Brothers and sisters, think of what you were when you were called. Not many of you were wise by human standards; not many were influential; not many were of noble birth. But God chose the foolish things of the world to shame the wise; God chose the weak things of the world to shame the strong."
1 Corinthians 1:26-27 (NIV)

God will choose the weak and transform them. There's no denying God's power when someone weak or foolish comes to Him and is transformed into a strong, wise child of God. Many are called by God, but only a few answer His call. God will call you to Him, but it's your job to answer the call. Don't worry about being strong enough or wise enough for your calling. As you walk hand in hand with God, He will transform you into what He's called you to be.

DECEMBER 7TH

God Knows What He's Doing

"The Lord said to Job: 'Will the one who contends with the Almighty correct Him? Let him who accuses God answer Him. Then Job answered the Lord: 'I am unworthy - how can I reply to You? I put my hand over my mouth. I spoke once, but I have no answer - twice, but I will say no more." Job 40:1-5 (NIV)

God can be very disruptive. He will come in and turn your life upside down. Life can get very hard, but know that God has a reason for everything. Trust God's plan since He is your Creator. He is using the good and the bad to mold you for a special purpose. God doesn't answer to you and He doesn't have to. He knows all things and He is working them for your good. Be quiet and allow God to be God. He's your Master and He is creating you into His masterpiece. Trust His process.

Work For The Lord

———◆———

"Whatever you do, work at it with all your heart, as working for the Lord, not for human masters, since you know that you will receive an inheritance from the Lord as a reward. It is the Lord Christ you are serving." Colossians 3:23-24 (NIV)

God puts you in certain places for a reason. You may not always like the way you're being treated in those places and feel like there is a lot of unfairness happening in that place. Don't focus on what is happening around you. Focus on Jesus and keep yourself from being distracted by all the chaos around you. Do your best work for the Lord, don't do it for people. God is the Big Boss in charge of all things. Remember that He is the One who will reward you in the end. His reward is far more greater than anything man could ever give.

You Are The Light

———◆———

"You are the light of the world. A town built on a hill cannot be hidden. Neither do people light a lamp and put it under a bowl. Instead they put it on its stand, and it gives light to everyone in the house." Matthew 5:14-15 (NIV)

If you fill yourself up with God's Word, love, and light, but isolate yourself from others, then no one benefits from it. God fills you with His light, but it's not just for you. He wants to shine brightly through you so that others who are around you may also find their way through the darkness. God chose you to be a light in this world. Shine brightly. Allow God to use you so that the people He has placed in your path will also benefit from the love and the light He has overflowed you with.

DECEMBER 10TH

Receive Blessings For Losses

———◆———

"Truly I tell you,' Jesus replied, 'no one who has left home or brothers or sisters or mother or father or children or fields for Me and the gospel will fail to receive a hundred times as much in this present age: homes, brothers, sisters, mothers, children and fields - along with persecutions - and in the age to come, eternal life." Mark 10:29-30 (NIV)

Sometimes God will lead us away from everything we know so that He can become our everything. Once God becomes your focus, He will add all that you need and more than you gave up. As He blesses you with more, you will also experience more persecution. As you are being exalted by God, not everyone will be happy for you and some may hate you. If you can handle being persecuted, God will continue to exalt you.

Seek God And Do Not Worry

"So, do not worry, saying, 'What shall we eat?' or 'What shall we drink?' or 'What shall we wear?' For the pagans run after all these things, and your Heavenly Father knows that you need them. But seek first His Kingdom and His righteousness, and all these things will be given to you as well."
Matthew 6:31-33 (NIV)

The ones who are not God's children will focus only on material things, but those who are children of God knows that if they focus on Him first, He will add everything else. He will never let His children go without. God will provide all that you need as you follow Him toward your destiny. Trust God in every situation and you will never feel incomplete. The more you trust your Father in Heaven, the more He will bless you with. He is all you need.

Live As A Believer

—◆—

"Nevertheless, each person should live as a believer in whatever situation the Lord has assigned to them, just as God has called them. This is the rule I lay down in all the churches."
1 Corinthians 7:17 (NIV)

God has given each one of His children an assignment. You may not always be comfortable with where you are in your life and you're not supposed to be. God doesn't promise to make you comfortable. He grows you through uncomfortable situations. No matter how difficult things get, trust God in all circumstances. Ask Him what it is that He wants you to learn or do in your current situation. The key to happiness is learning to be content with wherever God has placed you. He equips you with all you need to complete your assignment.

Secrets Of The Kingdom

"He said, 'The knowledge of the secrets of the Kingdom of God has been given to you, but to others I speak in parables, so that, though seeing, they may not see; though hearing, they may not understand." Luke 8:10 (NIV)

God reveals things to His children that others will not see, hear, or understand. He chooses who He appears to. After He shows Himself to you, everything changes. You will see Him everywhere you go. He will speak through people, through signs, or anything around you. The longer you walk with God, the more you will see and hear Him. People will not always understand what God is saying, but His chosen children will understand. Look for God and listen for God everywhere you go. He is all around us. Be open to seeing Him.

Whatever You Do Will Prosper

———❖———

"That person is like a tree planted by streams of water, which yields its fruit in season and whose leaf does not wither - whatever they do prospers. Not so the wicked. They are like chaff that the wind blows away." Psalm 1:3-4 (NIV)

Be careful not to do evil to get ahead. You may prosper at first, but eventually it will catch up with you and you'll lose it all anyway. Follow Jesus and He will teach you how to prosper. Don't get discouraged if things don't look the way you'd like them to at first. If you continue doing good work, the Lord will prosper you in His perfect timing. It's important for you to know that you can't sit around and wait for God to move. He's waiting for you to move first, then He will bless you with prosperity and bless whatever your hands touch.

God Can Do The Impossible

———◆———

"When He had gone indoors, the blind men came to Him, and He asked them, 'Do you believe that I am able to do this?' 'Yes, Lord,' they replied. Then He touched their eyes and said, 'According to your faith let it be done to you,' and their sight was restored. Jesus warned them sternly, 'See that no one knows about this." Matthew 9:28-30 (NIV)

When you go to Jesus for help, go to Him believing that He is able to do all things and that there is nothing too hard for Him. Jesus will heal and restore you according to your faith. Works plus faith is how you become successful. Your life will change completely when you put all of your trust in Christ. People who knew you before will have a hard time doubting the power of Jesus when they see how Jesus transformed you.

DECEMBER 16TH

Freedom From The Enemy

"Keep me free from the trap that is set for me, for You are my refuge. Into Your hands I commit my spirit; deliver me, Lord, my faithful God." Psalm 31:4-5 (NIV)

God will protect you from your enemies. He won't allow you to lose. He is your refuge. When your enemies surround you, God surrounds your enemies. He will deliver you out of the hand of the enemy always. Trust Him to go ahead of you and devour the enemies that lie in wait ahead of you. He won't allow you to fall into the traps of the enemy. He will warn you before your enemy attacks, but it's up to you to take heed of His warnings. He will give you a way out of your troubles, but it's up to you to take it. Praise, thanksgiving, and speaking God's Word are spiritual weapons to use against the enemy, so fight back.

God Calls All Sinners

"On hearing this, Jesus said, 'It is not the healthy who need a doctor, but the sick. But go and learn what this means: 'I desire mercy, not sacrifice.' For I have not come to call the righteous, but sinners." Matthew 9:12-13 (NIV)

Jesus came to heal the sick. He explains to the Pharisees that the healthy doesn't need a physician. He tells them that He didn't come to call the righteous, but to call the sinner to repentance. We've all sinned in some way. You don't have to be ashamed of being a sinner. All of us fall short, but Jesus called you to repentance and He wants to make you whole. Give Him your heart and accept His forgiveness. Allow Him to show you the person you were created to be in the Kingdom. It's much more peaceful and joyful allowing Him to lead you.

Overcome Evil With Good

———◆———

"Be not overcome of evil, but overcome evil with good."
Romans 12:21 (KJV)

You can't control what people do to you or how they treat you. You can only control your own actions. When someone does something to upset you, don't allow yourself to be overcome with evil or you will lose self-control. Whenever you lose control over yourself, it gives the devil a foothold in your life. The best way to fight back against evil is to overcome it with good. Whenever the devil attacks you, find someone that needs help and help them. Bless someone that is in need. Fighting in this way keeps you out of trouble and also allows you to bless the life of someone else. Maybe your blessing will even be what brings them into the Kingdom of God. Fight in the spirit, not in the flesh.

DECEMBER 19ᵀᴴ

Precious Cornerstone

"For the Scripture it says: 'See, I lay a Stone in Zion, a chosen and precious Cornerstone, and the one who trusts in Him will never be put to shame." 1 Peter 2:6 (NIV)

God gave us His Son, Jesus, to be our rock. Jesus is your foundation and it cannot be destroyed. He sacrificed His life so that you could live life to the fullest. He did not die for you to live a miserable life. God wants to give you an abundant life and He gave you Jesus to teach you how to live abundantly. Put all you have in God's hands and trust Him fully. He will not allow you to be ashamed if you give Him your heart and your life. Jesus died so you could live.

DECEMBER 20ᵀᴴ

The Lord's Instructions

———◦•◦———

"The Sovereign Lord has given me a well-instructed tongue, to know the Word that sustains the weary. He wakens me morning by morning, wakens my ear to listen like one being instructed." Isaiah 50:4 (NIV)

Life can be pretty draining at times. It can get a little overwhelming. That's why it's so important to wake up and get God's Word in you before you start your day. The more Word you take in, the easier it is for the Holy Spirit to guide you each day. God's Word not only refreshes your spirit, but it guides you daily. God's Word is the light that allows you to see your way more clearly to the next level in your life. Wake up with Christ every morning and watch your life change forever. God's Word will bring you and your family prosperity in every area of your lives.

Adversity Is Your Teacher

———◆———

"Although the Lord gives you the bread of adversity and the water of affliction, your teachers will be hidden no more; with your own eyes you will see them. Whether you turn to the right or to the left, your ears will hear a voice behind you, saying, 'This is the way; walk in it." Isaiah 30:20-21 (NIV)

No one on this earth is exempt from adversity. We all go through difficult times. It's the way you handle these hard times that really matter. You can see trouble and want to run away or you can see trouble as a teacher which makes you stronger. When trouble rises up in your life, be grateful for these teachable moments and know that this too shall pass. Change your perspective on the way you see your trials and adopt a fighter spirit. Get excited for the fight.

DECEMBER 22ND

Head Power And Authority

———❖———

"For in Christ all the fullness of the Deity lives in bodily form, and in Christ you have been brought to fullness. He is the head over every power and authority." Colossians 2:9-10 (NIV)

Before coming to Christ, many of us felt very empty inside. We felt hopeless, like we didn't want to live. We were waiting to die. But God, He stepped in at our lowest point and pulled us out of the darkness that surrounded us. He filled us with His love, light, peace, and joy. He put us back together again, one piece at a time. He made us stronger than what we were before. Then He gave us purpose. He gave us something worth fighting for. He fills us with His power and gives us authority over all evil. Through Christ, we have the power to change the world one person at a time.

DECEMBER 23RD

Apart Of The Royal Family

———◆———

"Someone told Him, 'Your mother and brothers are standing outside, wanting to speak to You.' He replied to him, 'Who is My mother, and who are My brothers?' Pointing to His disciples, He said, 'Here are My mother and My brothers. For whoever does the will of My Father in Heaven is My brother and sister and mother." Matthew 12:47-50 (NIV)

You may have to leave certain people behind so you can follow Jesus and answer His call on your life. Your family won't always understand why you had to leave them behind, but you know that God has called you to something greater. When you become a follower of Christ, you become apart of God's Royal Family. You gain more when you sacrifice what you have by leaving it behind to become what God has called you to be.

Acquitted Or Condemned?

———◆·◆———

"A good man brings good things out of the good stored up in him, and an evil man brings evil things out of the evil stored up in him. But I tell you that everyone will have to give account on the day of judgement for every empty word they have spoken. For by your words you will be acquitted, and by your words you will be condemned." Matthew 12:35-37 (NIV)

You will know if someone is good or evil by their actions. The way you speak to people or treat people says a lot about who you are as a person. Your words have power. Your tongue has the power of life and death in it. It's crucial to watch what you say to yourself and to others. You can't be good and evil. You have to choose which side you will be on and go from there. Which side will you choose today? Good or evil?

DECEMBER 25TH

A Savior Is Born

"She will give birth to a Son, and you are to give Him the name Jesus, because He will save His people from their sins." Matthew 1:21 (NIV)

Eve was tricked by Satan in the Garden of Eden. He told her that if she ate from the tree of knowledge of good and evil, she will know all things. God's command to Adam and Eve was not to eat from that tree. Satan came to trick them, and they did it anyway. When they disobeyed God, they were thrown out of the Garden of Eden. But God, He didn't leave us to suffer in darkness. He gave us His Son, Jesus. He was born to save us from this fallen world. He came to save us from our own sins. God's children will all be together again with our Heavenly Father in Heaven. Be sure to thank Jesus for His sacrifice for all of mankind. Merry Christmas.

DECEMBER 26TH

Coming Forth As Gold

———◆◆———

"When He is at work in the North, I do not see Him; when He turns to the South, I catch no glimpse of Him. But He knows the way that I take; when He has tested me, I will come forth as gold." Job 23:9-10 (NIV)

God will test you. He builds your character through trials, using them to strengthen you. You won't always understand why you're experiencing opposition in your life, but trust that God is working behind the scenes for your greater good. Everything that is on your mind, is in God's hands. He knows how uncomfortable you are in trials, but you learn the most about yourself when you are uncomfortable. After you have gone through the fire, you'll shine like gold. You'll thank God for allowing you to go through tough times because of the person you are today.

Faith In The Storms

"Lord, if it's You,' Peter replied, 'tell me to come to You on the water.' 'Come,' He said. Then Peter got down out of the boat, walked on the water and came toward Jesus. But when he saw the wind, he was afraid and, beginning to sink, cried out, 'Lord, save me.' Immediately Jesus reached out His hand and caught him. 'You of little faith,' He said, 'why did you doubt?" Matthew 14:28-31 (NIV)

The love of Jesus is calling you to Him by name. He wants you to walk with Him in faith, even when storms rise up. The storms come to test your faith. When things are getting rough, focus on Jesus. He will calm the storms in your life. The moment you take your eyes off Jesus, the storms will swallow you up. Focus on Jesus as you walk in your purpose, trusting Him to hold you up.

DECEMBER 28TH

No Longer A Captive

"You will seek Me and find Me when you seek Me with all your heart. I will be found by you,' declares the Lord, 'and will bring you back from captivity. I will gather you from all the nations and places where I have banished you,' declares the Lord, 'and will bring you back to the place from which I carried you into exile." Jeremiah 29:13-14 (NIV)

Many of us have been held in captivity by the enemy. We have suffered from pain, fear, worry, and anxiety. Sometimes we felt hopeless and wanted to give up, but God stepped in. He wants you to seek Him with everything you have before you decide to give up. The Lord is telling you to seek Him and you will find Him. It doesn't matter what anyone else is doing. Don't be a follower of people, but of Christ.

DECEMBER 29TH

Overflowing With Hope

"May the God of hope fill you with all joy and peace as you trust in Him, so that you may overflow with hope by the power of the Holy Spirit." Romans 15:13 (NIV)

When you choose to follow Jesus, you are no longer empty inside. God fills you up through His Holy Spirit. You become anchored in hope. Even when obstacles are placed in the path ahead of you, your trust in God allows you to become fearless and push past the obstacles that come to block your path. As you fight against the opposition that tries to keep you down, God will fill you up with joy which strengthens you and perfect peace through the power of His Holy Spirit. When you trust God completely, you can let go of trying to control everything and allow God to work things for your good.

DECEMBER 30TH

Honor God With Your Heart

"This people draweth nigh unto Me with their mouth, and honoureth Me with their lips; but their heart is far from Me." Matthew 15:8 (KJV)

God knows your heart. You can't pretend with Him. It's important to have a relationship with God. You can't depend on what someone else is telling you about God. Do your own studying. Your mouth may speak good about Jesus, but what are your actions saying? Will people recognize that you are a follower of Christ by looking at your life? Don't be afraid to let people know who your Father in Heaven is. You may fool some people with your lips, but God knows you. He can't be fooled. Allow God to come into your heart and teach you how to live. Ask Him to fill you with His Holy Spirit and allow Him to be your guiding light Home.

Purified In Truth

———◆———

"Seeing ye have purified your souls in obeying the truth so that through the Spirit unto unfeigned love of the brethren, see that ye love one another with a pure heart fervently:" 1 Peter 1:22 (KJV)

God has given you His Truth throughout this year to follow. He has given you a light to follow so that you can see your way more clearly. He has also given you a choice to choose to follow Him or not. To those who have chosen to walk with Him, He has purified you in His Truth. Jesus taught us through His Word to love one another sincerely. Love your brothers and sisters with all you have. I pray that going into this next year, you take all that God has taught you through not only your victories, but also through your failures. Allow them to become your teachers for the new year. If no one else has told you this year, I love you!

Printed in the United States
By Bookmasters